# LIGHT BENDING

## ALSO BY BILL NEVINS
(published by *Swimming With Elephants Publications*)

## *AWE*

### *Heartbreak Ridge*

# Light Bending

## Collected Poems of
## Bill Nevins

Sligo Creek Publishing Co.

Copyright © 2024 Bill Nevins
All Rights Reserved

ISBN: 979-89911983-4-9

Cover photo by Jeannie Allen
Cover and book design by Alan Abrams
Edited by Alan Abrams

Sligo Creek Publishing Co.
Silver Spring, MD
Sligocreekpublishing.com

## Dedicated to:

*Jeannie Allen with all my love,
to my children and grandchildren;
also, to Nana Anna Eagle—
and all readers with love and thanks,
and to the former night-manager of
The Golden West Saloon—
may they all live long and prosper*

# Contents

No Prisoners ........................................................................... 1
New Skibbereen ..................................................................... 3
Light Bending: Loinnir ......................................................... 7
Our Bernadette at Sixty ........................................................ 9
Tim Finnegan's Hod and Last Night's Fun ..................... 10
Anna Kiley ............................................................................ 13
Bad News, a Waltz ............................................................... 16
Saoirse Go Deo ..................................................................... 19
Columcille Adrift ................................................................. 23
Dearg Doom .......................................................................... 24
Elevator, 1966 ....................................................................... 26
Banshee Dance, for the Old Ones ..................................... 28
Iona, love ............................................................................... 29
Querencia and the Salt of the Earth ................................. 31
Gratitude—Momma Maia and Me .................................. 35
Una Limpia ........................................................................... 36
Undercover (for Marcial Delgado) ................................... 37
Desert Faith and Deluge ..................................................... 38
Atrisco Sunset ...................................................................... 39
Greasy Grass ......................................................................... 41
For Cactus Ed, Like He Said .............................................. 49
Black-Light ........................................................................... 50
Blue Flower, in a Vase, Perhaps ........................................ 51
Thorns, Blood and Verses .................................................. 52
Icarus in the Forever War ................................................... 53
Silence of the Messengers .................................................. 54
En el silencio de los mensajeros ....................................... 54
Carlotta's Prayers ................................................................. 55
Siete (Sing Her Name) ........................................................ 57
Awe (in the Dead of Winter) ............................................. 58
These Winds in September ................................................ 59
Mammal-fish, a chantey ..................................................... 60
Feather. Bed. ......................................................................... 61
Bill Morrissey, American Bard (1952-2011) .................... 62
Tunnel Rat ............................................................................. 64

| | |
|---|---|
| 1847 | 66 |
| after any war | 71 |
| Old Priests and Dotard Presidents | 72 |
| Reveille | 73 |
| Transub Station New York Daze | 74 |
| Shane Had a Wake, But Shane's A Wake | 76 |
| and so is the Snake | 76 |
| The Fire -Wall | 77 |
| Under Her Veil In Aurora She Eyes A Rainbow | 78 |
| Within the Silence of the Messengers | 80 |
| Eclipse | 81 |
| Cackle and Scratch | 83 |
| Widening Gyres | 85 |
| Dien bien phu | 86 |
| A Shadow of Cloud. | 87 |
| Limbo Rocka | 89 |
| After All | 90 |
| Gold Star Dirt, Cash and Glory | 92 |
| Patriot Graves | 93 |
| Lincoln County Road or Armagideon Time | 94 |
| A Curse in Time of Mourning, Rage, Angry Love | 95 |
| But You Promised Me Broadway Was Waiting For Me | 97 |
| Safe As Houses | 99 |
| Assouf | 100 |
| Afterburner | 102 |
| Dignified Transfer 2013 | 103 |
| Buy Me a Ticket to Ride | 104 |
| Heartbreak Ridge | 105 |
| Lá an Dreoilín | 110 |
| How They Do So Plan for Us | 111 |
| Worlds Open on Smokey Worlds | 114 |
| TAKE AWAY | 115 |
| I do | 116 |
| St Magdelene | 117 |
| Buddha's Wagon | 118 |
| Hirschman | 119 |
| Sonny Rollins | 121 |

| | |
|---|---|
| Jerry Garcia Done Gone Long Gone | 123 |
| Aiséirí | 125 |
| Brush/fire | 126 |
| White Castle is a Very Good Place | 127 |
| Waiting for the Hog Farm | 128 |
| to Serve Breakfast? | 128 |
| The Brink (Someday We'll Ride Again) | 130 |
| Cyberia | 132 |
| Boogaloo | 133 |
| Calavera Sunsets: All Remind Me of That | 134 |
| Canción | 136 |
| A Gentile Kaddish Sung | 138 |
| for All Fallen in the Sun | 138 |
| This Bleak Sadness | 139 |
| Coot Vicious in Memory | 140 |
| oh omar in darkness, | 141 |
| what the hell ya dreaming now? | 141 |
| No nuke is tactical | 142 |
| A Well Regulated Militia | 143 |
| Shane MacGowan in the Green Room, 1987 | 146 |
| Lock Up & Get Out | 148 |
| Kabul Sunset | 149 |
| Enough | 150 |
| Acknowledgements | 151 |
| Bio | 152 |

*The light was no more than a mean and taunting
reminder of what light could be, a rumour
of what light there once was.*

~Kevin Barry, The Heart in Winter


*The phenomenological world is not pure being, but
rather the sense that shines forth at the intersection of my experiences
with those of others through a sort of meshing into each other. We
know not through our intellect but through our experience.*

~Maurice Merleau-Ponty, Phenomenology of Perception


*In the end it matters, it's worth the fight,
We'll be damaged, there will be hell to pay,
Light after darkness, that is the way.*

~Jay Farrar/Son Volt, "Promise the World

# No Prisoners

What can I say?
We met in Santa Fe.

She's got everything she needs,
She's an artist
And she knew John Berryman.

Poets
are worse
than lawyers
she said
worse
than mosquitoes
Like those big flying cucarachas
down south
they get in your hair

Poets!
Poets tell you stories!
Stories about
anarchist painters
who won't take cash
from the cruel corporate state
so
they live in boxes
made of cardboard
under bridges
without berets
without brushes
without canvas stretchers
without grants
without patrons

without brushes

Poets
she said
are like syrup
on a pancake
they soak in
until they wipe out all the taste
of the pancake itself
and fill it in with words
words
words
sweet, sticky
words!
Poets make everybody else
taste
what they taste
she sighed.

I
hate
fucking
poets
she said

First,
she hissed,
after the revolution
we'll kill
all the poets!

# New Skibbereen

*Oh child, I loved my native land, with energy and pride*
*Til a blight came over on my prats, my sheep and cattle died,*
*The rents and taxes were so high, I could not them redeem*
*And that's the cruel reason why I left Old Skibbereen*
~Patrick Carpenter

So that's how they sang back in the bad old days, for Erin's sake.
And we all look back on the old country, with a yearning eye.
Everybody needs a safe place. Hike in the mountains. Swim in the lake.
Liam Neeson himself sang a bit of that song in that grand rebel movie Michael Collins.
And he's a fine figure of a man, and no mistake.
Seems the songs then were mostly about going away.
Now the Irish are welcoming the world and his wife back for the Gathering.
Now that they seem to have found Peace.
But "peace comes dripping slow."
You know.
This tribe's fire falls not far from the smoldering tree:
When we rage, swear
break up the crockery
It's not that complex or romantic
at root
It's not really about the whiskey
at all at all,
For all last night's fun.
The booze is just fuse
to the hard detonator charge
the i.e.d. if you will
as Yeats said
made stone by too long a sacrifice
in the weary world's flow,
the high temper, the warp-spasm
built up from scraps of sad memory
priests' empty plates
and icy hearts
nuns' despairing tears
and
shards of shattered love and pride

denied
through confessional repression, stake, jail, starvation and evictions
and home places
occupied, re named
re-christened, grabbed
by foreign capital or arms
or ideology
without due apology
and nearly forgot.
almost lost
beyond the Pale
of living memory
*Tiochaidh ar la*
Our day will come
Bobby the dying soldier- prisoner- poet, starving, hemmed in, gasped back in '81.
Another fine rebel movie that.
It's about space
About room
and Lord knows we'll put up with a lot of crowding
Like when the musty Roman Curia sends a wee priesteen
across the wine dark wild sea
to plant his bed in our own back room
invading once again our most personal space
and
he offers us in payment his lilting prayers
of healing, of patience, of acceptance, of accommodation
to our economic fate and the politicians and bishops' human errors
along with a quiet rosary, a Gaelic folk mass
collections for the African missions
hopes of clerical vocations and liberation theology
plus a recommended better diet, vegan no doubt,
with our blessings, after all, to count,
An Gorta Mor being so long buried in the past
and
potatoes glory be no longer scarce

thanks surely to our never eating meat on Fridays,
and always keeping the Faith..
Well, you know for all that,
it might have gone on as ever it did around here.
We were, after all, looking forward to The Gathering and lifting a pint in the bars
like everybody else
And at least we're not on Cyprus, thank the lucky stars,
But then the simple holy fool
went and tried to lift our secret Sile na Gig out of the ruined church wall
and there was stern comment
about that
in shaded corners no outsider knows exist—we'd near forgotten them ourselves in truth
Some stones shall not be moved—
and so
they found the poor holy young fella
mad as a goat
in moonlight
lost in some farmer's rocky field
in a faery circle in the County Cork
turning and turning
on his heels
in widening gyration
round and round
all alone
so very alone
muttering to no one his rescuers could see
about Cuchulain's smoking forked tree
and the four scorched severed heads up in its branches
he was very bad in his head
they said
yet somehow not quite dead
So
They led him away, and asked us to pray
for him and themselves.

And so.
On Paddy Day, even deep in glum Lent
We do pray for time
Time to pay the rent.
Time to plow and plant.
Time to rise one more time
at long last
aware.
Aware it's High Time to cease all this bloody useless prayer!
For it's coming on Easter now, boyo!
When we'll give off with their Latin prayers.
Stuff them under the dark back stairs.
and simply sing:
in our own vulgar native pagan unchurched dharma voice:
As lovely drunken Mangan sang,
as blind poet Raftery sang
as cutthroat queen Grace O'Malley
and Brendan Behan sang in every breath they drew
as Sinead O Connor, Damien Dempsey,
Shane Mac Gowan, Flann O'Brien,
Liam O Flaherty,
Padraig Pearse and Peadar O Donnell,
lovely Jim Sheridan
as all the banshees and colleens and Molly Malones
and even dear dead James Joyce on his best night
might have sung:
                    *Óró, sé do bheatha abhaile*

O, mother dear, I long to hear you speak of Erin's Isle,
Her lofty scenes, her valleys green, her mountains rude and wild
They say it is a lovely place to raise a laughing child,
So that's the fairest reason to return to Skibbereen.

                    *Gráinne Mhaol agus míle gaisciochag*
                    *fógairt fáin ar Ghallaibh*

# Light Bending: Loinnir

*for Loinnir, Roisin, Bernadette and the Revolution*

It's a long long way from here to Clare
Where white horses race ashore in salt and cold spray
And in the Doolin pub thick- bearded Aran fishermen
Draw long sips of black stout,
Gossip in the ancient tongue,
Wonder who the quiet Yank might be—
In time of sad civil war up north
I just sat, took breaths and stared
on a rock along the western shore
waiting for the moon to rise
or thinking vaguely of captive Roisin
far off in a London jail alone
and how I visited
her famous mom one day up in Tyrone
Yankee left journalist on walkabout
accepting a kind cuppa tea—
They'd asked if she was bitter
these many hard years on,
as was rumored.
"You know the thing I can't forgive
is that these wee ones
didn't grow up in farm country
with all the war
and all the war
for
we had to raise the three of them
here on this stark city ground
just to breathe at night
just to stay alive"
She sighed

dreaming perhaps
of flower fields, hills
and cattle horses dogs
with a running child free by a laughing Irish river
"Well, you know,
I had longer hair back then,
not this Ulster matron's Peace Process do,
and they said i was bad then,"
she smiled,
"But I'm worse now, far far worse!"
Then our wee rebel Bernie
the miniskirted firebrand of Derry of Belfast,
of the hall of Parliament and the English jails,
who saw the paratroops deal out murder
that awful Sunday in seventy-two,
now herself a gray granny,
took her new grandchild
home out of foreign captivity
and told all us nosey press about the kid's newly christened name:
"Loinnir"
"It's a ray of sunshine,"
she said,
"Not the bright summer glare
you might imagine,
but Loinnir
means the pure rare sunlight
as it filters down through even the darkest of clouds."

# Our Bernadette at Sixty

IN 1969, that Ulster gutter preacher
Ian Paisley himself
with his Yankee doctorate from Bob Jones U,
unsmiling, with his dirty money salted away,
with his imperial law
and his gunmen in the shadows
called herself, twenty one years old,
"Che Guevara in a mini skirt"
(Her tresses flying free on the Derry barricade)—
*That* right windbag of a bloodstained bastard—
where in hell is *he* now?

*Bua nó bás* growled hard lads, lasses
in pubs, prisons, dole queues—
Big Ian's bombast unfunny to the likes of *them*—
Seven bullets in her and she still had a laugh to share
Ya like my peace process 'do?
she smiled, touching her coiffed grey hair
showing off a snapshot of her kids
You know the thing I can't forgive
is that these wee kids
didn't grow up in farm country
as we'd hoped
with all the war
and all the war
for we had to raise them in here
on this hard black city ground
just to stay alive
just for them to live
she said dreaming of flowers, fields,
cattle, dogs and sheep and
a running Irish child by a free Irish river
I had longer hair back then,.
Yes, I did,
she smiles,
but I'm worse now—
far,
far
worse

## Tim Finnegan's Hod and Last Night's Fun

*Anam mac an dhuil!*
*Do ye think I'm dead?*
~Finnegan's Wake

One unremarked morning
you catch your old fella looking back
long after his funeral
through the clean-polished
mirror in your bathroom
With odd white hair
sprouted on his face but still Himself
the very man nonetheless
bare-knuckled short- tempered bad- ass Navy chap
with your same names, first and last
Looking out at you happy enough:
no trace of grave chill, cancer
or the bad deaths he saw at war front
or home front
nor any anger—surpisingly- -at long last
only . . . puzzlement.
He starts singing for sweet jesu's sake—
A ramblin wreck from Georgia Tech
And a helluva an engineer!
Singing!
Like a Glenn Miller banshee in William F. Buckley's
last dearly paid for Latin choir
Et cum spiritu tuo—
Oklahoma, West Side Side Story, Belafonte
DAY-ME SAY DAY-A-A-A-AAA-OOOOOOOOOOOO!
and
of course

the Wearin' o' the Green
Now come tell me Sean O'Farrell Tell me why you hurry so?
You wake there and then in the morning shower,
with yer awld one humming Tommy Makem, Bali Hai or Bloody
Mary's Chewing Beetle Nuts,
to the revealed Truth
that
we can leapfrog
bad times
evil deeds done and suffered
even pain and horror sites
shrinks be damned!
thoughts or feelings unwelcome
air brushed away—celluloid on the floor
like they weren't
meant
to be
in this final cut
like Hitler never happened
like the bomb never dropped
nor funerals
nor carrier decks aflame
nor finding an ancient Tipperary lady
charred and still on her lace-curtained Connecticut kitchen floor
nor original sin
nor fists in a child's face
nor sleepwalking off the double-decker roof
nor divorce
nor cold Pennsylvania rain

outside a locked heart and a screened porch door
Edit one's own life movie—
you can, y'know—
as if you were Cassavetes, Jim Sheridan, Woody, Penny or Jean Luc
and why the hell not?
Over arching Mercy—believe in her or not—
saw we couldn't rightly bear
the full raw picture
and so
gave us this gift
in fulness of time
to be enjoyed never feared:segue one good flashing scene
straight on into another
and remember only
Last Night's Fun.
It's like that eerie concert when Miles turned his back on us—
an old school Black priest to the humble congregated—
and held one beautiful aching note for what seemed all night long,
never looking
at any single one of us
but piercing every soul:
Ite, missa est:
Gwan, this mass is ended.

## Anna Kiley

Anna Kiley came out from a family of nine
on a farm in Cahir in County Tipp
somewhere at the end of the 1800s

she lived a century, wearing her good farm wife's dresses
and singing her great grandson Molly Malone
a Detective Sargeant's mother in law,
she oten took the bus from Stamford to Bridgeport
to visit relations with never a fear
We lived in one of those fine old two story houses

next door to the Ukranian seminary enclave St Basil's and I ran
free and wild as a child

I would fly upstairs in my Superman cape
for tea and cookies with Anna and her daughter
even when I'd knocked over my mom's best vase
for no anger, however righteous

could touch me sitting at the checkered kitchen table,
the fine afternoon light slanting through the curtain lace
singing cockles and mussels alive alive o

Anna died in a fire
and no one could save her
just as I began my teenage years
her farm wife's sleeve caught an open flame

as she tried to make tea
one last day alone
the wake was a grand event
they all say
I only cried for forty years or so
wandering manys the street broad and narrow

this wide world o'er

Delaney roared whiskey driven New York City nights with me

settling his own haunted dreams
with girls song and rebel disregard
of the church or Catholic fear
"Ah Billy look right into her eyes, man,
She wants you to see how pretty she is"
and his sly hand and smile
more often than not

found a way between gently coaxed thighs

all Ireland did arise
and we danced down Manhattan's
streets of fire and rain
laughing off our pain
and singing songs of Ireland
in the Bells of Hell

while Malachy held joyful court

and the Ballad of Bernadette Devlin wafted from the juke
The Bogside exploded and I hit Dublin

just as the Brits were dragging folk from their Belfast and Derry hovels
to prison ships and the Republican University campuses

you know the long story
the war and the glory
Paisley's vicious bluster
and the Women of Armagh
volunteers cut down in Ulster
or on Gibraltar
mother of sweet Jesus
weeping

as, locked in a NYC cell on a street that Mayor Dinkins named
after him, Joe Doc played the

barber for wise guys and kept the flame lit
or dear Roisin hauled off pregnant to a London hell

or

McGlinchey man and wife riddled
or Scatter O Hara in a lousy Dublin jail
or all the mourning

or all the peace doves in this new morning

at last
at last
but down all those years
the anger and the tears
I always heard the wheels
of her ghost rolled barrow
bringing me home
to Tipperary quiet nights
a jar in the pub
and singsong
till the dawn

# Bad News, a Waltz

Like speaking words of love to a bad drunk,
Batting a bear with a black-
iron fry pan
is decidely
counter productive
it makes no dent
Or as the grizzly told Tim Treadwell
I ain't no metaphor man
were he simple vermin, beyond human pale

wolverine

or some snake tailed slithering giant New Guinea rat
and were you not already dead, Tim

even you
might set a sharp trap
snap his scrawny back
like UB40 ska-jive--
stag o lee neck snap--
simple as that
But he's
Grizz, man,
long gone gray
grumpy in moods
brave enough in his day
rears up on hind legs
still
now and then

plays deadly chess with Tony Hopkins
if you credit movie hype
bearded, big-shouldered, brawny, hirsute
and oh so tragically stupidly

male--

what that cool Kraut cinemage
saw safe behind time and a long lens

cold-eyed Grizzer red in tooth and claw,

Pilgrim,
basso profundo rumbling
snuffling
growling, piss drunk
shambles
through
our kitchen at night
lonely enough to gobble a man

whole

cough, curse, crash into her table
the kid's high chair

howl out my name, your name, his wife's name, mine,
cracking her new glass coffee pot.
Of course he never meant--
how could a bear mean?--
any of it
at all at all
in morning light
just trying to get sober
enough
shuffles big feet
slurps black java
scalding
so cuddly when he's sweet
big dark bear
his ragged yellow hooked paw
groping for chips,
cold pizza
hand rolled tortillas
all that rich hot food she'd put
away in the fridge hours back
when he didn't come home
all garbage to him now
well fit for him to eat
snuffling through it all
while she pulled a stoic blanket over ears

not to hear
that damned bear
in her pantry
once again

How to mend the damage done?
Buy her a steel Mr. Coffee carafe
dog house roses
join AA, find God
get a job

take her out for truffle fries and fine white wine?
Yet how to get that bear out of her kitchen?

Ever?

He ain't no Teddy. No Papa.
He ain't no Pooh.
He ain't one bit funny
and he damned well can't be YOU!
How To forget terror?
How do you get bear outta kitchen?

Don't shoot the poor damn bear.
Just never let the bastard back in.

# Saoirse Go Deo

Graffiti on the wall
It says we're magic
We're magic
Graffiti on the wall
It says we're magic
Up the Celts Up the Celts!
So went that Wolfe Tone song
They used to belt out at the Boston
Noraid steak rackets
I thought I'd cross the water
Back to the old sod
And take a first hand peek
Some four generations on
at the magic writing on their walls
And we say, Hoo-hah Up the Rah,
Say Hoo-hah Up the Rah!
So Ireland dear land was like Larry's song—"An American
Wake":
Land of my Gaelic mothers
and stern Fathers
where
You can always go home
but
You just can't stay
Gerry Adams himself told me he hadn't been to the coast of
Clare
in a long long time
and wished he could go, that busy, busy man
I nursed the hangover those Ardoyne lads had arranged for me
on the bus up from Dublin
and fumbled with my tape recorder
clumsy Yankee reporter
in a place I didn't belong
and my mind drifted off from my questions

Lapping of the Atlantic waves
Never a curse on any soul
They couldn't lift
with sit
stare at the horizon
slow breath and salt spray
White horses chased ashore
Dark clouds pushed in from the off islands
Shark fishermen in their old boats
Black tams, beards and woven jumpers in the pub
"Don't snap their pictures Mishter Yank
Unless you know them"
And you don't
Gossip in the old tongue
Sipping the black stout
I was there in time of feud
"planet of the Irps"
(when such jokes still flew)
or
"Divis hang gliding society"
ha ha ha
but wisecracks didn't fly much in those days
they'd become serious times
Cops let the old lads out early
1987
Sly constables they
are you see
Held the young turks back a while
then let them caged birds fly
Rat tat ta tats—gear and dope flying too
up and down the dirty towers of Divis Flats
While them peelers laughed and sneered,
"Up the Feud, lads, Up the bloody Feud!"
Settlin' scores and takin hostages—
a mother shot dead bathing her babes—
"Mishter, I wouldn't go up there alone if I was you
Show yez around . . .
If you'll take me picture, then?"

Touts, turf, Brits, In-laws, PAF, CRF, IPLO and Rah Rah Rah:
Say Hoo-hah Up the Rah, Say Hoo-hah Up the Rah!
Belfast's own night of the long knives to lull the noisy kids to
sleep—
Saoirse Go Deo and Peace Through Superior Firepower
the grim graffiti on those dark walls in this dark hour.
Must confess I didn't find much magic in Belfast
nor anywhere in the Occupied Zone,
at all at all—
Not one faery ring any place near their rusting Peace Wall
only Willie Yeats's refrain ringing in my head:
"Come away human child
To the waters and the wild

For the world's more full of weeping":
Bernie and her daughter looking like all the grief of Eireann
with Dom McGlinchey's coffin on their shoulders
and all the funeral parades
all the fear, all the wailing
all the brave soldiers loyal to their sides
fighting the good cause
dying for the good cause.
Scatter,
the Tommy Gun hero of Derry
in times far past
now a slight man
sitting in his lousy Dublin cell
trusting no one near
feeling hard the drawn-out deaths of comrades
some he brought on himself
the torture never ending for him
at home or away
Asking Boston to send software—
no more guns
"I'm studyin'now," he says,
Waiting for release.
And I went back to the Doolin shore,
sipped a few more pints with the shanachies and Germans,

waiting for my plane
remembering bold Seamus Ruddy's name—
that bright lad I had met in NYC in 1981
when Bernadette came on crutches after she'd been shot
and Seamus toting a guitar case seemed more to be INLA
security than a stage entertainer
we chatted long and hard about the Mountbatten attack
and other matters of war peace and death
Besides Joe Doc he was the most informed and intelligent Irish
rebel partisan I had met and I liked
the man though we disagreed on that operation and much else.
As a Yank, I could only offer my outside opinion.
He was in the thick of the war.
A few short years after that, bold Seamus Ruddy disappeared in
France
Killed by comrades so the rumors went, over "gear."
For refusing to tell them what he didn't actually know.
Perhaps they did not mean to kill him. But they did.
His grave was hidden, no pleadings made its location clear.
listening for the waves- song
waiting for release
waiting for our day to come
waiting for freedom
waiting perhaps
for ever
Then some thirty years on in 2017
they at last found Seamus Ruddy's bones
in a hidden grave in France
and so his family brought him home to Ireland
at last at last

To paraphrase the great poet Paul Muldoon
whom I admire and aspire to imitate at times
and who wrote a fine poem mourning his own friend Seamus
Heaney:

> *I cannot thole the thought of Seamus Ruddy dead*
> *I cannot thole that thought too well at all, at all*

# Columcille Adrift
*Kolbjørn Columcille on All Souls Eve[1]*

*Beatus vir* began the great book
That he wept to read, preparing his boat
Return being much more than unwise
after so many good men slain–yet,
Great **Kolbjørn** yearned to hear aloud those psalms
long muffled in coarse Pict wool
*to undo the blood- spill, to be absolved*--
his pious foe's gilt sheaves of prayer
stashed in this rough pilgrim cloak
the blest and cursed scholar of God
who warred for words
wandered penitent, lost, wild
with blissfully unlettered Caledonians:
their dancing ways roiling whiskey pots
lithe hips red daggers tangled tresses
staked heads and shattered teeth
brought wan smiles to a sad old thief
for these wolf- folk knew neither saints
nor gold nor holy seasons
nor to fear Christ's tears
nor one syllable
of Romish verse held crystalline
in this Black Bear's mad trap of mind:
dreaming Iona on that smokey sea–Oh!
*If ever* the poets would gather there again!
Bards scattered, his prayers were never sung.
Where Norse waves lull fallen suns to cold sleep
from all desperate fires of wakened day--
silent, unshriven, the bloodied Dove drifts home

---

[1] The 7th Century CE Irish monk/poet Columcille, repentant for the blood shed in battle over a beautiful illuminated volume which he craved, went into exile to the island of Iona and thence to the Scottish mainland (Caledonia), where he journeyed deeply into the wild lands of the "pagan" Picts, who nick-named him Kolbjorn, "the great bear". Although he was posthumously glorified as St Columba, it is uncertain whether Coumcille ever returned home. His monastery on Iona was later sacked by the Norse Vikings, who burned many treasured books.

# Dearg Doom

*And when the stars fade out, you can hear me shout:*
*Two heads are better than one…*
~Horslips, "Dearg Doom"

Yankees sit on their arses and clap, but Paddies be jumpin'
on the seats and tables! We enjoy ourselves, so we do,
quipped Joe, not a year out of Long Kesh, building rock gardens for Doolin hostels.
keeping the lads at McGanns smiling with a song or a tale.
"Aye, when we came into the blocks, the hard men there made us sing
every damn rebel song we knew. If you missed a line you had to start
all over again. Ended any fear you might have of the screws, for you knew that lot of
hard lads were with you through thick or thin. We needed that, being locked up and all.
So we did."
Fairy forts where no farmer moved a stone. Bare ruined churches with no roof for wind
nor rain, Sheela Na gig in the stone church walls never to be moved.
Joe took me all about that wild West Clare land, up the Limavady back road in 2nd gear
and down to Lisdoonvarna for the fair where the auld fellas look for brides.
Ah his mad black-eyed beauty sister trying to find her way in the dark—
mind the bogs, mister Yank—darker than winter in Donegal!
Out to Spanish Point where Christy Moore's sister welcomed us warmly, as Sean said

she would, and asked how Barry was getting on in America
with his new name Luka Bloom and a fierce long time off the
drink.
Stumbling home from one of the three fine Doolin watering
holes where the shanachies
told stories and lithe German girls gave the Temperance fellas
good reason to venture
down the pub—despite too many bodhrans being badly
banged—I heard a weird low
sound in the fog: "Banshee or Dearg Doom himself?" sez I to
myself.
Sure, though, it was only Brown Bess, Charolais herself a wee bit
lost on that moonless
Irish night, just like me. And we both made it home, so we did.
Ended any fear you might have of being locked up in this world
and all.
So it did.

# Elevator, 1966
*for Terence Hegarty*

Hey Dublin, how's about ye, then?
all our kids well grown
you're re-reading Frantz Fanon
up near Boston and me in Albuquerque
re-playing Rubber Soul—a Yankee continent apart
and still we recall
you were so well-read then
and sweet jaysus could you rhyme!
Sonnets come and go, come and go
but still we, Winch and Angelo
laughing at grim catholic stations,
statues, confessions and graves.
Delaney declaiming Carlos Williams
while Suzanne nursed Jamesons
one Lions Head day in New York City
and I recall that lower east side slum top morning
seeking lost Brooklyn lights
and the staring eye of god—
sure, weren't we the lot?
that time we almost got shot
Morningside Heights nineteen sixty six
on the serrated edge
of smoldering Harlem
when the elevator steel shut clack
two shaking wretched of earth kids
wanted dirty money so bad
the hammer clicked back
blue steel 38 barrel at my temple
rounds at eye level

But it's never the moment
you thought it might be—
some say you never hear the bullet knock
but that wee gun-man flinched,
a mere shadow of himself
and we all went back
to that hazy beatnik party:
"Isn't it good, Norwegian Wood?"
Fifty years are gone by,
Would ya believe that, man?
Send me your new songs
whenever you can

# Banshee Dance, for the Old Ones
*Raramuri South Valley Marigold Parade, 1999*

Dancing up Isleta Boulevard, wrapped in the Tricolor of her raza cosmica,
smoking a cigar, singing her nasty chola blues—eagle waltzing the serpent home—¡Viva Las Muertas!
Mystic warriors challenge spirits to sing, to tease los niños to laugh.
reminding us "Irish Indios" of our fallen dead, woke again, like Padraig's pagan children.
not quite in heaven, yet never fearing hell.
Limbo. Where the unbaptized babies and the decent pagans go.
Listening for that ringing bell. Laughing in the sunset. Dancing in the dawn.
Wasn't it the truth I told ya? Lots of fun at that mad warrior Cuchulainn's wake!

# Iona, love

We were the brats of the good war's heroes off to study verse,
accounting, marketable skills
in a prosperous peace time turned spinning war time that
confused us no end
raised on Fulton Sheen, now Cardinal Spellman's blessed
nightmares, we donned dark shades, scapulas and dodged Mass
and the Stations all out in the wide world on our own at last
Catholic masses working our way around classes future cops
saints battle vets n poets
ragged right yet we fit into George's and the Beechmont and all
the Bowery bars
somehow mob that we were
ringing the profs up from a Village dive
to come down and lesson us when they could
sorry we missed your lecture today, man—
there's a cold one n a hard shot waiting for you here—
maybe a warm eye in a short dress as well—
truth to tell,
they sometimes even showed up—
and borrowing *Seven Types of Ambiguity*
and never bringing it back to George Little that gentle scholar
and loosing Panthers and Yippies and bright women onto your
holy ground
shards of gawd and revolution for the promising heaven of it
glory be
had to think Darby Ruane, good showman, secretly admired our
pluck and gall
what with Paul Delaney dancing on his one good leg, smiling
through his mustache,
a knife stuck into the other wood shaft a drink in his hand there's

a good laugh lad
whiskey yer the divil—Bells o Hell ring a ling ding a ling,
and Terry Heg composing soulful sonnets and that fella in night school Don who the hell?
So many songs we sung that music never died, brother, never will,
weather warrior hiding in the library, true,
and that sweet brother daley dean of discipline red faced two fisted but knowing not what to make
of tie- less disrespectful hirsute boys in black howling Jewish Buddha poems
in his sacred Spellman Hall while wee girls giggled all a gog
and Dean Quinn good man dancing that jig
when the old brigade blew Nelson ass over tit in Dublin
and not many of us could figure why but liked seeing the stern old chap cut a caper
and all the ladies of CNR
learning etiquette
sharing soft Glen Island acid dreams, letting kisses be stole as they would,
and stealing us silverware wrapped in white linen for our hovels
and drinking smoking us tuff sailorlads under the table on a good night's
ramble out in dear dark dirty blessed
New Rochelle

# Querencia and the Salt of the Earth
*On the high road to Chimayo*

Querencia is a safe place
from which one's strength is drawn;
a place where one feels at home.

Home.

Our common land, this land, our homeland, was free
In the time when the jaguar, elk and bison roamed
And those bravos Indios hunted free and prayed to the wide sky.
In the time when those good indigenous folk welcomed
Our peaceful ways into this land.
Despite the horrors
Of conquest and enemy- raids they had suffered.
Despite our having been exiled from glorious Santa Fe
Sent to these mountains bearing only bows and arrows, pikes and scythes
To face *Los Comanches* armed with rifles supplied by Anglo traders.
So we could with our children, with our bodies, guard the
haughty Hispano rich and clergy
Who nestled in comfort around their Cathedral of the Holy Faith.

For, not soldiers, we were workers and farmers and detribalized
*Genizaro* co-defenders
Of this shared frontier land.
*Camaradas. Compadres. Compas.*
Not *los pinche conquistadores* from across the ocean sea.
We had thrown off those royal chains.
¡*Orale!* ¡*A-ho!* Blood in Blood out!
Homies till the wheels fall off.
¿*Que no?*

Then the gringoes came.
In their wagons, in their trucks
In their dozens in their multitudes.
Singing their cowboy songs
Singing their rock n roll tunes.

It was our sacred privilege then
To fish, to hunt, to graze, to gather wood,
From river-bed to the high snow ridge
And beyond to *los ejidos*.

Now we own little land, little wealth,
Little but our dreams,
Our skills. Our pride our faith
Our families, our *verguenza*,
Don't you see?

These latter days,
Enchanted, beguiled,
or befuddled
by history,
We are still free.
Free to be rolling out of these dear hills
So we might pay those "blessed" bills.
Cut some timber
Build a house, string a fence
For those who came here,
From good- Lord knows where

To live. To breathe clear air.
To pursue their own . . . happiness.

We will haul them pinon
and fine oak
Well-split,
To warm their winters.
We do not begrudge them
Their pursuit.
Their answered prayers.

We have precious little.
But we give what we have
To give.
They give
what they
 will
give.

They brought the great productions here:
Movies to shoot by day, by night.
On the high points above.
Their klieg-lights blaring,
On the ridge we all once owned.

Now a *rico* rents them that spot
Where his mansion is planted
For a very high price.

Yet, in the film crews,
We now work,
For good pay,
 *¡Gracias a Dios y Jon Hendry y the UNION IATSE!*

Yes. We are strong union- folk
Now.
*¡En solidaridad!*
And so, we may re-build
Our Querencia.
Here in this land
Of *los manitos* bravos.
This land of the brave.
This land all may own,
One fine day, fenceless, together.
In community.

This enchanted land.
Where our children may study law, or sing our holy songs,
Pursuing their own, long- delayed, dreams.
Pursuing their happiness, don't you see?
In this dear Land that once was,
and so will be

Free.
Even when the fires and floods sweep our lands
And the FEMA drags its federal feet.
We are patient.
Oh so patiently we wait
For we know those who wait
Shall yet rejoice
In due time.
So we give thanks
For all that shall truly be.

For the lion screams in the barranca
And our souls here are always alone.

# Gratitude—Momma Maia and Me

She never asked my name,
though I may have guessed hers.
And YES, you betcha I stood in awe of Nature
when that angry momma elk—
six foot tall and counting—
silently charged me
one early New Mexico mountain May morning
as I'd been distractedly strolling
contemplating abstract poetry,
fallen leaves and vague signs of bear
in the forest edge of Elk Poop Acres
(no doubt too near her hidden newborn calf)
She had precious little to say about Yeats,
Ocean Vuong or Emily Dickinson
but I got the message most clear
about my own mortality
and fragility and her fierce desire
that I just get the fuck outta there
fast
and I got the picture
of the size of her stamping hooves
not five feet away
(the wise dog ran home)
ah yes, I was grateful
for a tree that day,
nature's gift, me behind it,
(as I am grateful not yet to be dead)
standing stout between me and that proud lady elk
and more thankful I was still
when my own brave woman,
much bolder and wiser than I,
gracefully turned that elk away
with a hurled stick and a shout
so that grand creature left me
and sauntered away into the woods,
her white rump and regal disdain
blessedly bidding me
to have a nice long life.
I grudgingly wished her the same.

# Una Limpia
## *(Burque Daze)*

Cleansing the memories of peeling chiles, stringing ristras,
Celebrating the iguana and Santana
I wend this road many years on
Whistling gabacho gypsy over the hill
Knowing that there may be no fond Spanish goodbye song
As Stephen Dedalus remarked in "Ulysses,"
"We walk through ourselves . . .
But always meeting ourselves."
And I remember those tears,
Those laughs—Ay, dios mios!
Those South Valley sunsets
The waking to chicken crows and the question,
"Scrambled or juicy?"
The ghetto birds buzzing
Bullets tapping the tin roof
Of a New Years Eve or Independence Day,
The black widows lurking, pitbulls lunging,
Tequila shots, weddings, funerals,
Mad dog stares, black berets, smokey mota,
Flaunted bling, hidden guns and enchiladas
Slinging hay bales, breathing soft through warrior sweats,
And failing to learn how to make adobe bricks
The funerals and the healing ceremonies.
The curandera's poetry, mad as midnight.
The limpias and candles lit for the newly dead.
The prayers that were said as all prayers must be said
Gracias a dios y la Buena cosenada
panza llena, corazon contenta
Can't complain.
¡Sé que nunca fui verdaderamente familia, en fin, mi amor!

# Undercover (for Marcial Delgado)

*Ain't no money in poetry, that's what sets the poet free,*
*I've had all the freedom I can stand.*
~Guy Clark, "Cold Dog Soup"

Behind mad dog shades, or an icy stare
Behind rhyme that rolls in a low-slung line
While your blood pumps fast in street-smart time—
Hey, poets, in this fine land of hope and glory,
How's it goin'? What's your cover story?
Your cover could be a killer or a lover
But a glass heart hides in a steel-onion sheath
Where the poet waits to be a gift-giver or thief.
A poet could be an agent of destruction, or reconstruction
Could be hate and fire, could be love and warm desire
Could be a friend you never knew. Could be an enemy gonna wreck you!
Could be what you need to share. Might be your worst lonely nightmare.
Poetry is an art where . . . sometimes you get to pick and choose . . .
But poetry is that thing you just can't lose—
Open up—your mind— your ears—your heart!
Pick your verses and poets like you pick a good pair of shoes!
They gotta fit! You gonna get hit by the poetry you choose,
Poetry is an exchange—you get the lines you pay for
And, trust me, poetry ain't free—Oh no! You gonna have to pay!
In love or blood or beer— or just with an open ear.
Y'see—Poetry is a buried treasure—that's for damn sure,
You gotta dig for it, y' dig?
And poets don't ever just fade away.
Poetry is here to stay—Americkay!

# Desert Faith and Deluge

*for the Water Protectors and for the Mora Valley*

When she calls to us from ancient farmlands
from holy plains from the brave river,
she calls to blue sky stripped trees wind ripped clouds.
Grey cliffs shrug to feel the weight of rain, of ice, of sun,
to hear her cry.
We answer her with howls of coyotes, bird calls, rustle of leaves and pine needles
or with the silent laughter of stars.
Our wise friend says we take in too little water here.
Rain courses through our sleeping bodies until lightening
scorches and wakes our souls.
We must fuel that torrent that flash.
As our eyes storm when we see her dance, hoping she may
drench us in forgiving tears, so revolution flows in a turn of her hip.
Yet we stop, stone-dead,
without that river run sea swell ocean roll.
We know this too well.
We all need that reservoir. Great gulp. Small sip. At least enough to spit.
At least enough for the next kiss.
For we are that odd legged-fish wrenching itself up into this new dry day
in this place where a forgotten god meant us to be all along but dared not tell us,
for we could not imagine the feel of dirt
suck of lung stretch of limb
what it is not to swim
in wavering shadows with the sure pull of the moon.
So we dream of dolphins, seals, whales and lonely selkies
who sing us our own lost memories of that sweet wave-rocked
life soft lullaby of time long gone, before this place of stone
became our always home
under a hard fire stare under an icy star glare.
It is so dry here.
In this desert town, let's taste her tears, those wild, roaring glacier streams.

# Atrisco Sunset
*A Christmas Salud to Don Juan Rey de Noel!*

Like their pretty women the beers of the Germans
On that European tour Don Juan Rey took, courtesy of LBJ,
Were pale, cool, filled with hidden delight:
Every Deustch burgh served up its best
To a rock n roll G.I. and a journeyman barber
Who joked *en espanol* or *ingles*
And tried to gaze into every new friend's eye taste every rare brew
So far from old Nuevo Mexico so far from home
So far from mother dad *hermanos y hermanas vatos y amigos*
Learning all he could so far from all he knew
Gone awol a few times tasting Europe's hidden delights
Learning words tastes songs all fresh all new
Sharing their good company, his smile, his dry Atrisco laugh
He won many hearts and minds for NATO for Nuevo Mexico for Atrisco,
His barrio hid in La Resolana by the bosque— which few in the great wide world knew:
Old as its deep dirt, cool as its alamo shade
On this holy ground of his abuelos, abuelas, Don Juan Rey rode his proud John Deere,
Tilled and nourished his fields down all these long short hot cool years since then,
Where the *grujas* cranes soared and gathered in spring, fall
Where his brothers sisters son daughters *primos y amigos*
In laws outlaws and even the odd visiting *gabachos*
All hoisted heavy bails from his fields up to Don Juan Rey's *trucha*— hook and sweat!

Honest labor in the old way of this familia, this tierra, this pueblo.
After that hard sun soaked work they still sip good American Buds or perhaps Tecate
With smiling Don Juan Rey who remembers the clear rare beers, warm eyes, sights, songs and hearts of Europa far away, far away.
Rejoicing in Don Juan Rey's birthday *de Noel*,
We sing Las Mananitas, taste his carne adovado—the best!
After mass this Christmas Day, we toast his life his *ninos ninas* grandkids nephews nieces
His good crops hard work warm words jokes and quiet smiles and
We toast again his joy his dark Dona, the true bright love of his life
We honor and envy his memories his joys:
Don Juan Rey's clear beers, Don Juan Rey's cool and sparkling hidden delights.

# Greasy Grass

*for Wes Clark, Jr. for Phil Crazy Bull,
and for Jorge and Sandra of The Raramuri Center*

Long-Knife bugles sang their strange song
along the Little Big Horn
The People in their thousands woke to a warming spring day
Crazy Horse and He Dog laughed as brothers laugh in battle
And caught their war horses on the greasy grass plain
Buffalo Calf Road Woman prepared her rifle once again.
Blue coat soldiers fell into the camp, confused,
as Sitting Bull had foreseen in sun-dance vision
and they lost their ears to hear
"The Garryowen's" glorious lilt
or the bugles and the orders roared out
by that Yellow Hair Long Knife colonel
who smoked the holy pipe with the Cheyenne,
vowing peace
and lied like a dirty dog
The Northern Cheyenne—they rose
The Lakota—they rose
The Dakota—they rose
The Arapaho—they rose
They rose to battle to protect their people
The Crow and Arikara, Long Knife scouts,
also rose to fight alongside the washitu
for that was their honor and that was their fate
That day along the river of the greasy grass
Where fifteen thousand horses grazed
Many fought. Many counted coup.
Many fell.
Now memorials decorate the hills east of the Little Big Horn
Thousands visit in the summer heat, they say
I visited when the ice had recently broken in the streams
and the winds blew chill
Aho! Mitakeye Oyasin! All my relations!
Come all ye and hear my song!
Made brave by brown eyes
glinting around the lodge fire,
I toss my red prayer bundle into flames.

Bare bison skull hangs above fire rocks.
Deep in South Valley Burque, Isleta and Rio Bravo.
Raramuri, place that honors prophecy, place that honors their story.
Ghost warriors rage
in their ancient tongues.
I ask in my poor Euro speech:
Who won the war? Who lost?
They never answer.
A strong-scarred woman xicana shaman
requests
That all the glowing stones
be brought in at once
And doused with sacred water.
So we may sweat.
So we may sing.
So we may pray.
Steam rises and my breath is strained
While I lie flat on the lodge floor
trying to suck cool air from beneath raw-hide walls
and my wise friend Jorge lying beside me
laughs at my plight
Deep voices rise in chorus around me,
and my shy self, desperate to sing along too,
Gasps in poor Irish, Tiochaidh ar la—our day will come.
But they know not my language, kin, clan or tribe.
As they swirl around me on their painted ponies
Neither fully dead nor truly alive.
Yet where did the triumphant day
of these fallen warriors go?
Far far away in time, space and kind,
They ride a war path, mad for joy, mad for pain.
Yet here, today, in this hot place in this weary mind,
As Bob Marley sings in my own reaching brain:
Rise up fallen fighters,

Rise and take your stance again
Tis they who fight and run away,
Live to fight another day!

I strive to touch these wraiths.
And talk only with myself:
No past life crap here, amigo.
No peyote dreams neither.
Your own "ancient ones" crawled off an over-loaded coffin-ship
bound to Americkay from starving Connemara.
Stern Protestant greeters let your starving relations off that horrid
plague-boat
On condition that the refugee women, kids and Catholic clergy
kept quiet
while all able Irish men volunteered to fight for the Yankees'
rippling star-striped flag.
The paddy-recruits relished the meals, guns and saddles provided
them
and soon grew eager to whistle that rare old tune of "Garryowen"
so beloved by their preening Yankee General with the curling
yellow hair,
he who "looked like a king in command"
on his bold white dancing stallion.
Sure the Little Big Horn would be a fine day in the sun!
We know who won that battle
at what the Lakota and Cheyenne
called Greasy Grass
One fight won, though, is not the war,
And these ghostly indigenous warriors
have years of hard tears—tales to tell, sorely earned.
Sitting Bull and Crazy Horse ride alive—only in memory
summoned up by the lodge- fire's glow.
Blue-coat steel and lead felled their noble bodies.
Long ago.
We sang a round of that old Lakota chant for the lost bison,
Wonka tonka!
Skin drum throbs while steam chokes my throat.
Old gringo war dogs wake and snarl:
"For all their victory feasts and sun dances—We returned!
With Christian vengeance, smallpox, Hotchkins guns and sabers,
We returned,
And then!
We settled scores."

Buffalo soldiers, renegades and the Seventh Cavalry rode down
their screaming wives kids and elders.
Trampled their lodges and tents.
Left their wounded bodies to freeze.
Eighteen Ninety.
Wounded Knee.
A hard century later,
vision-poet John Trudell, of the Santee Sioux,
sipping tea in a Taos Poetry Circus bar,
spoke up simple and plain:
"We're using ancient songs, my friend,
to sing to the about-to-become-extinct,
If we want to get right down into it."

A black-eyed poeta
stepped up to that bar,
laughing at me and all our motley poet crew.
She sang in bright Spanish and bold Nahuatl
and then again in shabby Ingles.
She sang us them old dirty blues:
¿Quien es tu amante?
Nimitztlazohtla Noyollotzin (nee-meetz-tlah-zoh-tla no-yoh-loht-seen)
"Just who may your lover be?"
As the chants rise and steam blisters the face.
As the fierce shaman dies and lives again.
Yuwipi.
One heart. One voice. One chanupa,
That holy pipe was passed round
to the Prophet Crow Dog,
Heir and avatar to Crazy Horse,
Who had hacked his own black braids
in mourning
For a son who had married badly
and died hard by the knife.

A smug British historian laid out plain the case for white
aggression in his book
The Wars for North America:

We Euros needed land for our starving masses
Huddled in steerage, transported,
Fleeing tyranny, false religion and the rich,
Bringing clean new faith, fear of Jesus, and that great motivator,
Greed, a profit motive
From our tired old lands to their fresh new lands—
The Sioux, the Cheyenne, the Crow, Comanche, Dineh,
the vagabond lot of them,
like bloody Mongols,
they just wanted to gape at the sky
worship the wind,
fly along with bison herds
pronghorn antelope
eagles
sun and moon and endless wild clouds
Over those plains so lovely.
Those plains so gone.
Paint, beads and bear claws!
Teepees and cradle-boards!
Feathers in the breeze.
We needed that place.
We needed those plains, those hills.
We needed that rich dirt.
That silver. That gold. That iron. That water.
That glowing stone. That wealth.
That uranium.
We need that Power!

Those shabby Indios had to go.
With their odd medicine.
With their Ghost Dance and Ghost Shirts.
They had to go.
Far away. Back to the reservations, back to the cursed bad lands.
Back where they came from, treaties be damned.
This was a land rush, and divil take the hindmost!
WE needed to hunt!
WE needed to fish!

WE needed to homestead.
WE needed to MINE!

We might leave them our good books
We might leave them our Christian churches,
We might leave them our haircuts and suits,
Our whiskey, our casinos.
Our smallpox.
And our cancer. (So said that Sandhurst military professor, greatly respected among his peers.)
The grieving holy man called down black tornadoes—
On the children of those who did black murder at Wounded Knee!
Twisters these latter days, do come more and more.
Kansas bled, then Oklahoma Texas Mississippi Louisiana
—terror on the Gulf Coast Shore. Hurricanes in New York!
Earthquakes, lightning and thunder.
And all the USA is afraid again, it seems.
Building walls.
Strung out on scag and meth and television dreams.
Dreaming of vengeful mushroom cloud towers.
Dreaming of when America once was so great.
Dreaming of those good old days.
Before refugees, immigrants and dark-skins
came and took it all away.
That kind brown woman asks why so rough
—with such a soft voice?
I have no words to tell her
what my ghostly horse-soldiers moaned in my mind:
"Our rifle butts broke their bones
But their war-clubs beat us down.
Our scouts and troopers died—
Boots on, battle-flags streaming.
Bugles blaring the Garryowen blues."
Instead, I draw a breath and pray:
These ancient nights,
new big sky days,

Hand in hand,
May we touch once again—
peace in our time
Aho!
My dead Long-Knife auld ones growl one last fading growl:
"We came into their camp by night
Light of fires moon gleam of sabers,
Singing,
'Where ere we go we spread the name
Of Garryowen in glory.'"
Then. There is silence.
Silence at last.
I have no ears to hear.
Those damned old cavalrymen retreat
from my mind
and dissolve back into hell or nightmare,
or whatever world may claim them.
And my own voice returns,
breathing slow and free
in quiet prayer:
Breathe once again
Hear once again
Touch hands
again
perhaps one last time.
Hum "The Garryowen."
So softly. Silently.
In mind.
In peace.
In light.
And that is the End of my story.
But the story goes on.
May we all wake
from this dream
this dark story
not to dread
but to glory.

Aho! Mitakeye Oyasin!
All our relations.
The people feasted, danced, then struck their lodges
Crazy Horse stopped fighting
And he was killed by bayonets
The people moved North to Canada
As the wise ones suggested
Many winters came
many summers
Many children were begotten
Sitting Bull and many old ones died
many young ones came alive
Custer's bones were dug up and buried back east
The Greasy Grass Fight never was forgotten
The people live on.
Wounded Knee.
Standing Rock.
This holy place here.
Right here.
They live and they remember.

## For Cactus Ed, Like He Said

*Better a cruel truth than a comfortable delusion.*
~Edward Abbey

desert rose desert fell
desert was a great big swell,
a salty old sea, those snakes that swim,
they can tell:
when the waters fall or rise
       when the last desert rose will fall

# Black-Light

We see dimly in this new war-time.
ML King was shot through his neck.
We are not the parents we dreamed,
We are merely the parents we were.
We imperfect live on.
Those perfect young are dead: your daughter, our son
We see the young march again to the Somme.
We see the old men sell guns.
We see light in young eyes.
That last glimpse before death.
We cling to the last sight of age.
We don gas-masks perhaps.
Night vision goggles.
Facebook personas.
We see war, fog, blood. Here and there.
We see. As a blind sniper might
Raging against the failing light.

# Blue Flower, in a Vase, Perhaps
*we see today that we shall surely die*

the children sing as they mourn
their murdered peers laid beneath,
those dull bullets in their eyes,
fierce joy on their lips—their sharpened teeth!
they waste no more time as fear's slaves
they march, they plant seeds, they dance—
they will tramp down dirt on the NRA's graves
I would leave you perhaps
a blue flower bent in ice water
a song to sing as the night draws near
when we have no more money, no more day
when the hungry children take our last breath

## Thorns, Blood and Verses

*Como no me he preocupado de nacer, no me preocupo de morir.*
~Federico Garcia Lorca
*Eisenhower has touched hands with Franco, embracing...*
~James Wright

On Christmas Eve this year,
Federico Garcia Lorca bursts, laughing,
from the pavement in front of Trump Tower!
El Maestro declaims on CNN—

> *Poets, like thorns, make us feel!*
> *Poems, like blood, flow.*
> *Poets' blood may flow*
> *Poets, like roses, may die*
> *And disappear into the earth*
> *So more thorns may grow*
> *So more poems may flow.*

Alarmed, Trump and Stephen Miller
fly to Spain on Air Force One
to lay a Christmas wreath
on the grave of El Caudillo Francisco Franco.
Before the New Year dawns,
Rats nibble the wreath away.
Franco remains *extremadamente muerto*.

# Icarus in the Forever War

*For Matt Ho and Keith Sherman*

He loved the wild sky, wanted to fly.
He fell out of our time, left us here, behind.
His brave true-love parachutes under an African sun,
Her dreams of him forever haunt dry hills of Afghanistan.
Steel Magnolia women honor heroes tumbling into a dread political maze
While impatient families count out the endless mission days
A loyal sister climbs in Alaska snow
to pitch her memory-flag under aurora borealis glow
as another sister circles female hearts
in the moon and star's turns, wishing for his return,
that never will be, while his Gold Star mom
misses no wreath-lay holiday nor any war-jet salute
roaring over his cold Colorado grave.
Soldiers do as told. Generals let them die—they must comply
with El Presidente's orders. Clinton and Baby Bush, after all,
started this mess, like Midas. And Trump just grumbles and
fumbles along. He too, will die.
Obama was a much politer killer. Surgical drones, as Hillary
advised.
We all liked his cute kids. He just seemed so wise.
Maybe some new President will come along and end this bloody waste,
Get us back to good old days, okay, fellow boomers?
if we just keep faith, vote well, slap steaks—or tofu burgers—
on the grill on Memorial Day
and the Fourth of July. None here dare ask why.
His father just piles a rock cairn under blue Sangre de Cristo sky,
searches for fallen feathers, beneath a vast indifferent heaven.
Daedalus did not cry. He had even more hard puzzles to try.

# Silence of the Messengers

We hear only hush of wings
these angels who
sweep around us
never a word spoken
never a sword drawn
though their voices be strong, their hearts brave,
knowing we would not remember
if they spoke
would not remember one soft word
nor recall one fiery blow

so we greet them only with heart
beats as is the way of our kind
as is the way of this unknowing mind

# En el silencio de los mensajeros
*Translated by Fer de la Cruz*

Oímos solamente el murmullo de las alas
de estos ángeles
que entre nosotros vuelan
sin pronunciar palabra
ni blandir ningún arma
aún sabiéndose dueños de voces portentosas
y regios corazones
pues saben que
si hablaran
no lo recordaríamos
ni quedaría conciencia de la menor palabra
ni del más fiero golpe.

Por eso solamente
los percibimos con corazonadas.
Es la única manera de nuestras mentes desconocedoras.

## Carlotta's Prayers

On a Gulf Coast Yucatán beach road near el muelle—
the pier in Sisal—
Don Angel proudly displays his well-kept moto-taxi,
a canopied motorcycle with seats attached for passengers,
the sort of vehicle that is often a cab for hire here.
But his cab is far more than public transport,
though he will give you a ride in courtesy
if you need to travel to the flamingo lagoon or the octopus beach.
No, his vehicle is a shrine which honors and celebrates
the glorious life and brief reign of Empress Carlotta of Mexico,
delicate daughter of King Leopold of Belgium and grieving widow
of Holy Roman Emperor Maximilian of the Hapsburgs,
who tried in vain to rule Mexico Lindo when French bayonets held sway.
You see, this Holy Emperor merely wanted to bring good government
and reform to the pious Catholic people and pagan souls of this troubled land
But alas he became instead "a bag of bullets"
when Napoleon Trois lost interest in his sovereign claim
and the Indio Presidente Benito Juarez harshly restored the
Mexican Republic.
It was she, royal Carlotta, who ordered a stairway built
down into the beautiful blue cenote on the Hacienda Mucuyche
where so many campesinos toiled to raise hennepin
and where so much alcohol was distilled.

And she did see that stone staircase carved.
And she did dip her lovely royal feet in those mysterious fresh waters,
even though los indios, stuck in old superstitious ways, said, "One should never bathe there!" For ancient ones are in the waters,
buried there in honor or sacrificed to please the fierce Maya gods who might not approve of a visiting lady from Europa, however refined,
dipping her dainty toes into their sacred pools.
Yet, poor devout, faithful Carlotta lived on, in exile and asylum, long after her dear Maximilian was killed.
Many deemed her mad because she never admitted that he was dead.
And so, these 150 many years along, Don Angel in his moto-taxi sings her praises,
despite her madness. For are not the saints all insane in their mad love of Christ?
As he roves the sandy streets of Sisal in rain, in heat, in wind and in chill.
Don Angel knows Blessed Empress Carlotta prays for him, for us, in her heavenly
chambers far above. And one day the dear Holy Father may declare her sainthood.
So, Angel grows old, and yet he is assured that all is and ever will be
in glory, and that this most holy world is without end, amen.

# Siete (Sing her Name)

*And all they will call them will be . . . refugees.*
~Woody Guthrie

Uno, Dos, Tres, Quatro, Cinqo, Seis, Siete . . . They lost count
They saw so many, so many walking up this way
To El Norte to Los Estados Unidos to Gringolandia, to peace.
From Guatemala, from Honduras, from Salvador, from Mexico,
Bolivia, Somalia, Syria, Iraq . . .
from more lands than we can count, from more pain than we can feel.
In la resolana, by the American Wall, they gather.
Asking for our help, asking for a place of shade, a place just to rest.
They put her in jail: no food, no water, no help.
She was one of hundreds, one of thousands.
There will be millions more. She was one.
She counted seven years. She will not count another Christmas.
She died of hunger, she died of thirst. She died.
In a border jail, in this United States, in New Mexico—she died.
They lost count of her among the hundreds, thousands, millions
whom they do not care for, whom they let die. Whom they let fall
into the hands of ICE.
That frozen heart. Those cruel hands. Those concentration
camps. Those graves.
She lives in her father's heart, in her mother's cries, in her family.
In those hundreds, thousands, millions of families uncounted.
She lives in our quiet horror while the fat president worries
not about her but about his wall, his border killers
and . . . his money . . . his money . . . his money.
Among these millions coming to us, weeping, wailing, pleading
with us—
We sit in the shade and we speak softly of her
who died of the sun who died in dark. Who died
We may pray. Or we may scream. Basta Ya. Enough.
No more deaths. No more.
¡Siete! She is seven. She is dead. We do not know her name.
We may have no right to know. Yet we imagine we know her
name. We whisper her
name. We sing her name in our tears.

# Awe (in the Dead of Winter)

*For Buddy Wakefield and Ram Dass*

Why cry on the first of May
For snow and a melted holiday?
Those days caught in the old snapshots
Are these days. They are today, not then.
They are all one, they are all now.
Kids and flowers. Hills and rivers.
Nostalgia is a bore—waste time,
dreaming of some other then
that is no more? Be here now!
Old man's quip—it's now when.
Your smile, tears, shock at being seen now, and again:
My laughter behind the shutter, here behind my own eye.
Your eyes that sunrise. Aw, it's how it is.
Awe! It is. We are then, as we are. Now.

## These Winds in September

It's how we measure what we imagine is passing
Leaves fall winds turn chill —when he fell we all went a bit mad.
Words like shrapnel, words like ice scattered and sliced.
When he died perhaps we scarcely cried—at least we might have cried more.
Ah, those words spit in anger, rage, despair still sting.
This far in, though—it's been six years! Will we grimace and growl forever?
He'd have laughed it off. Why shouldn't we laugh, too?
None of us live longer than our time. Some of us live better than our times
I'll always keep his smile with mine. He was better and he was wild.
He was our brother, he was our child.
Hope you ride the same wild winds that he rides.
Hope you're smiling, too, when you reach his side.

# Mammal-fish, a chantey

*For Lord Franklin and his crew*

Mammal-fish, will ye swim here where we shove ice aside,
Fearing leopard-seals, orcas, cannibal harpoons?
With our wains facing fire ashore—Ah, damned if they'll quietly starve!
There shall be War. Red war. Bad on land, worse by sea.
Ye shall succor us shall ye not Dear sea-hag, mo chroí?
Mammal-fish flippers, teats and fins, will ye mother us home,
to Atlantis, fair Lindisfarne, Findhorn, Vinland the Good, *Tir na nog*—
That far, fair western shore that Arthur and Brendan left us all for?
Califas or the fine new Peoples Republic? Any decent port in this dark storm?
Mammal-fish, will ye crawl back ashore to "learn" us forgotten lore,
show us how we may breathe anew like whales breeching true, and rediscover—if it be
the blinking stars' wills—our faith in forgotten flippers, in lost holy ghostly gills?

# Feather. Bed.
*for the Sandhill gullas cranes, for us, for the flying for the landing*

circling in here spiral down careful now got to lower the legs
hold the wings steady turn the feathers down so down just so
mind the trees hey—watch the bushes for coyotes, crazy people,
fierce bears, a
momma elk defending her calf
ah yeah touching ground ah yeah touching down ah yeah
your arms wrap round ah yeah land
never quite imagined in my bird brain
it could be here this dear place never saw that far ahead
circling so long spinning mind spinning heart spinning dizzy
for all the mad view you know we land we do just so

# Bill Morrissey, American Bard (1952-2011)

*One more round, bartender—pour a double if you can.*
~Bill Morrissey

Never met you, man, though I lived in that granite ribbed Live Free or Die land,
like you, before I got Enchanted all to hell out here with enchiladas, Spanish eyes and
Desert Solitaire.
But I knew from your songs that you too felt the angels' lucid starry pain.
Yet I didn't know you'd died until this past November when I checked your "online tour
guide" and found obits on your site, Bill, beside cool pictures of you with your axe—older
and younger, long hair or trimmed, where Greg Brown posted oddly comforting agnostic words of little faith, tipped his floppy Whitmanesque hippy hat
to your literary taste. Seems he'd not seen you in too long a time nor gone with you, fishing for silver trout or picking golden apples of the sun.
And now he never will again, with you, Bill.
Some asshole of a critic said you "looked ill on stage." What with the drink, the road,
fifty-nine thirsty waking years, lost loves and all that sad song stuff you wrote. Sure, life
might have tasted like ashes in your whiskey sometimes, Bill, but the straight story goes that you just went to sleep alone down south.

In a motel after that last gig, the night before you were to visit
treasured friends.
Must have been a warm July night. Must have been a soft
blanketed bed,
a decent Georgia fit. And you dreamed of her mystery, her warm
eyes, long before this
year's winter snows would spit down on them quiet roads of Old
New Hampshire, as the
truck's tanks drained dry, and those north-flowing rivers would
run to black ice.
Sitting here hearing your songs, I feel that eternal sting, that chill:
"Fire on the ocean,
thunder on the sea."
I play your fading cassettes in my battered truck deck— "Robert
Johnson." "Handsome
Molly," "She's That Kind of Mystery," "It was the smoke that
killed him, not the flame."
I play them a dozen times in this cold New Mexico night,
weeping an old gray poet's tears that just might say, "I'm more
than some half-drunk,
burned-out god-damned fan who never met you, brother Bill,
just as you were so much more than just some eloquent, old-time,
gravel-voiced guitar-
toting beatnik-poet-drunk."
You were a pal, man. You are a friend of mine, Bill.

# Tunnel Rat

*For Captain Richard Flaherty, US Army Special Forces combat in Vietnam, KIA back in the USA. RIP*

Ain't no soldier, me, and I don't go where I can't see.
But, Rickie, you went in where no other Yankee could
or would to the dark inner hell of snakes, spiders, spikes,
where "law" was pistol, knife or tooth. Neither side dared use grenades
You came out alive, each time. Victor Charlie rarely did.
They made you a Captain of those Green Berets, not jumping from the sky
but wiggling underground: Vietnam. A war you never started. A war you might not have
understood.
Kill or be killed was what you knew, like Jack London's bloody-fanged hero-dogs
In those stories we loved.
Now the smug coward President fakes a photo op with a real tunnel-war K9 hero
and basks in unearned glory for his dumb ass lazy "base."
Somebody—we don't know who—killed you, Rickie, killed you dirty. Like a dog.
But, you were a MAN, Rickie.

I remember your smile passing in the halls of our Connecticut
"Catlick" high school,
1964: green blazers, ties, shined shoes. My hair flopping in my
face,
ruffled by hot girls that I feared. Don't know if they scared you
too, Rick.
You had the bravery, man, just to look and be looked at back.
So far back in the dim memory-mists.
Doubt we ever partied together.

Both of us were pretty shy, but you were a good guy, not tall but
perhaps the biggest of
us all.
Don't let them say otherwise. Don't let them say any damned lies.
Now, you're dead. But, you got yourself a movie (Like me).
Committing War.
Committing Poetry.
We went different paths, very different ways. I hope you had your
very good days.
Good night, dear brother that I barely knew. We all love you.
Walk clean, fly free.
Softly now, please shut down the lights, Rickie. Stay safe.

# 1847

*For Jonathan Harrington, Fer de la Cruz, Malachy McCourt
and Sean Hennessy[1]*

Sipping Oaxaca mezcal in Sean Hennessy's elegant Yucatan pub
on that Merida boulevard named for conquistador grandees,
built on ruins of the ancient Maya city of T'ho—musing, a bit
tipsy, on the mystery of
history—dreaming of 1847—a century before I saw my first light
of morning—the year the
Irish call "Black Forty-Seven" for the horrors of
hunger and eviction
Inflicted upon them by the cold heart of Imperial Britain—
munching fried potatoes to sop up the alcohol, I delve into
Oliver Reed's fine book *The Caste War of Yucatan* where I learn
that Black '47 was the very same year the Maya in
their thousands rose across all the Yucatan peninsula
with machetes and firearms in
hand to take revenge three hundred years on
for invasion, theft, rape, slavery, desecration of temples,
burning of codex histories, and vile disrespect to their still-hungry
gods. Indeed!
Rallied by their balam jaguar-priests, their battle-hardened
commandants and their
General Jacinto Pat, the brown Mezuhual "loincloths"—
Los Indios Bravos, as they were
called—slew their overlords—the "pants-wearing"
city-dwellers—white Ladino, brown

---

[1] During the American Civil War, Confederate States Army Company I, 8th Alabama Infantry Regiment, included 104 of its 109 men who were Irish-born. These men wore dark green uniforms; their banner was a stars-and-bars Confederate flag on one side with a full-length figure of George Washington in the center. The reverse was green, with a harp, shamrocks, and the slogans *Erin-go bragh* (Ireland forever) and *Faugh-a Ballagh* (Clear the way). Union Army Irish Brigades recruited by General Meagher of the Sword carried similar flags and also used Irish battle cries. Both sides included Irish speakers, and they fought each other, to the death. John Doyle has a fine song about this tragedy.

mestizo—men, women and children alike, without quarter, taking few prisoners except as
enslaved "spoils of war."
On jungle trails and at the gates of Merida and Campeche cities, the risen Maya tossed severed heads back at their enemies, set great haciendas a-flame,
sniped from trees and pyramid tops,
heaped stone blocks to barricade and besiege, just as their ancestors had done at the
time of invasion so long ago.
Then, the triumphant Mezuhual danced in fiestas to celebrate victory and to give thanks
to Jesuchristo, his holy santos and his Speaking Cross, and also to their many fierce,
undying gods of old.
Both sides—Maya and colonists— had their deities, their priests, their santos, widows, martyrs and slaves.
As is ever the way of war, both sides had their lines of supply; Spain's Cuba colony and the Republic of Mexico armed and fed the Ladino armies and
gladly accepted captured Indio slaves in payment, while British Empress-Queen
Victoria's profit-minded subjects in Belize sold the rebel Maya modern guns, powder
and ammunition, taking payment in looted goods and treasure.
In that same year 1847, many Irishmen, who had fled starvation at home, were pressed
into the United States Army for President Polk's land-grabbing war on Mexico, where
churches burned and nuns were raped. Many disgusted, maltreated Irish Catholic
cannoneers and riflemen deserted the Stars-and-Stripes army south of the Rio Grande.
They joined Mexico's Foreign Legion under their own green Saint Patrick banner.

Marching to the tune of "Green Grow the Rashes-O," they earned the fond nickname
"Gringos," and fought to the last as the San Patricio Battalion, famed in legend and
song.
Yankee bullets, whips and hanging-nooses stopped the hearts of most San Patricios
when Chapultepec Castle fell and Los Niños Héroes lept to death rather than
surrender. The US Army called them traitors and deserters, but Mexico honors them all
on September 13 to this day.
Connemara-born John Riley, the San Patricios' commandante, escaped execution but was face-branded with "D" for deserter and whipped by the American drumhead courts-martial.
Some say he fought another day in Yucatan against the Maya and for the Mexican
Republic. Some say he sailed back home.
Some say he stayed on in Veracruz. Some say he died drunk with the old soldier's
blues. Some, like singer Tim O'Brien say,
"It matters not if you win or if you lose."
So. It. Goes.
The besieged Ladinos of Merida and Campeche towns appealed to Washington, DC for
help against the risen Maya—they offered to give all Yucatan over to the gringos, if US
Marines would repel the pagan barbarians at their gates.But the Protestant Yankee
President, Polk—too busy stealing California, Colorado, Santa Fe and Taos—declined
this tempting offer, in part because he foolishly thought that El General Jacinto Pat,
(whose Mayan last name means "small fish"), was one of that despised Papist Irish

race! Polk wished no more bloody strife with rebel Paddies.
Scorned, the Yucatecan
whites turned to Napoleon III of Imperial France and welcomed
his surrogate Emperor
Maximilian and his Empress Carlotta to their shores—
at least, until El Presidente Benito Juarez cut short her "glorious"
reign and peppered
her husband Emperor Maximillian with bullets.
The fierce free Maya, in their Republic of Chan Santa Cruz
sheltered by the eternal Yucatan jungle heat and rain,
fought on for fifty years. They were guided by their Speaking
Cross—the Ceiba, the
Central Tree of the World—
until machine guns, betrayal and compromise ended their
sovereignty. That cross still
speaks to the Maya Cruzob,
In all seasons, wet or dry, to this very day, affirming the truth of
the Ancient Ones.
Not even the great Mexican Revolution silenced its voice.
None in the Cathedral town of Merida, or in the political center
of Ciudad de México, nor
even in raucous Cancún, dare say it nay.
Not even NAFTA, nor los narcotrafficantes nor El Presidente
AMLO, nor the crooked,
armored cops of Quintana Roo
have dared to try to silence its mystic voice.
And in Chiapas the modern Maya evoke Zapata as they rise up in
arms and long for the
coming of their own fine, free, peaceful day. So . . . it goes.
And so, I sit, an oddly-quiet Norteamericano, seeking history's
elusive clarity, munching
poc-chuc, sipping xtabentun and Jameson's laced with Chaya, at
Hennessy's holy altar,

this lazy January Sunday afternoon, with chattering ex-pats, poets and turistas all
around. Here I lazily dream . . . of Erin's green shamrock shore, of wild horses waves
racing in on foam, of sad John Riley all alone in a bar in Veracruz, of brooding jungle
pyramids at Chichen Itza, Edzna, Mayapan and Uxmal, of Jacinto Pat's shotguns,
flintlocks, rocks and machetes, of the tears and prayers of besieged women of Merida
and Campeche and the Maya strong-holds, of the dream of a free indigenous people's
republic, and of those dying rebel's last sad toasts:
*Tiochaidh ar la*, our day will come. Let the fight go on!
And I wish them all *Slan agus beanchta, Vaya con dios, hasta luego*—and more power to
their elbows, under the gloriously-crossed tricolor flags of Ireland and Mexico, draped
near the bar at bold Sean Hennessy's Irish-Yucatecan Pub, In Merida, Yucatan, this
grand sunny Mayan winter's-day.

## after any war

years now after the war
it never ended, by the way
no parades here—
and he was buried
with cannon-salutes and pomp
he would have hated—had he been there
but . . . he wasn't there.
he might be in the clouds he might be in the sky
he might be in the smiles, tears, laughter
the sighs of his friends, mom, sisters, nephews
in my own mad mind or in this beating heart,
he might still be here, really, all these years.
        after that war

# Old Priests and Dotard Presidents

Jesus, will you all lighten up already?
Diagnosis at distance is dangerous!
Forgetting how to say "Anonymous"
In front of a crowd
Does not mean you have dementia
Any more than forgetting
You are a fascist stooge
Makes you a winner
Or any more than
Abusing children for your kicks
Or locking them up away from their folks
Makes you an amoral sinner
If you can just
Forgive yourself
Forget what you've done
And build that Wall
You keep talking about
Clutch those rosary beads
And the Body of Christ
That you love . . .
Hang onto your lovely
Thinning hair . . .
Confess.
All will indeed
Be well.
Forget about it.

# Reveille

This morning
Early
light
Touched
your face
Then
Without
vengeance
We
Saved
The world:
Dawn

# Transub Station New York Daze

*Oh, now in this age of confusion*
*I have need for your company.*
~Richard Farina, "Children of Darkness"
*For Paul and Suzanne Delaney,*
*and for Lorenzo Duran and Lorcan Otway*

Those whimpled Connecticut nuns wondered
why I shook, sniffling
outside St. Mary's confessional box
when Father Fenton in his stiff Jansenist cassock
found me wanting in dogma, flunked me at First Confession
and
tossed me out of Holy Mother Church's embrace and
sent me
slouching towards Times Square
to seek faith and forgiving eyes.
When I got to the City
Ed Sanders tossed me out of Peace Eye Bookstore
just because I asked for a job
and then there was
just too much crystal-meth at hand
and Elephants Memory was not yet the Plastic Ono Band
that Summer of Love when the local mafia hoods
crushed a flower- power couple to pulp
for undercutting their set price of pot
and
that tough-talking girl from Montana
bells on her long dress
held my hand all one icy LSD night
as Prince Dylan crooned "Peggy Day" on WBAI
and we fell into our long opium dreams,
not knowing which prophet
we should doubt anymore
while the weather-folk chanted *ho ho ho chi minh*
and the cops grumbled and biker pipes roared
as fabulous furry freak brothers duck-walked down Avenue D

and a white bluesman on a flatbed rolled up Fifth Ave,
claiming he'd got his questionary and was needed in the War
and I put my gauntleted fist through a tenement hall window
just to hear it crackle forevermore
as we crashed hard digging Blonde on Blonde
slugging cheap Jameson shots and beer
while the skyscrapers flowed and the E train glowed
and a hot pizza slice left skin hanging from the roof of your
mouth
until
some late afternoon in St. Mark's Church
Eileen Myles or Jim Carroll might have been hosting poetry night
when
I heard Allen Ginsberg sneeze
in the middle of his Om Padme Hum
just loud enough
to assure us
that Shiva would
indeed
someday end our world
so
a further consciousness might grow
always so always so
it seemed
in the lush drone of his
smug soothing mantra

## Shane Had a Wake, But Shane's A Wake and so is the Snake

*Slán agus beannacht*
~Shane MacGowan

On the morning Shane MacGowan slept
All Ireland's saints and sinners wept
With that lovely aisling green-eyed girl.
The priests were hushed, dust unto dust,
And all the whiskey in this sad old world,
Like a proud piper's rising skirl,
Flowed, and flowed, and flowed.
Oh the words that Behan spoke
Seemed the wisest of philosophies
There's nothing ever gained
By a wet thing called a tear
When the world is too dark
And I need the light inside of me
I'll walk into a bar
And drink fifteen pints of beer
MacGowan flowed away, they say,
Holy mother mo chroí,
As the Tao flows, he flowed.
No pain, Shane: *Tiochaidh ar la!* Our day will come!
But the Nation's gonna rise again! And so may Shane—
Like Finnegan he's gonna be sippin' gin again!
Saint Shane straight outta Tipperary,
And a wild rake laughing at the Gates of the County Hell!
So name me a street and I'll name you a bar
And I'll walk right through hell just to buy you a jar.
A punk a Pogue a Pope a poet
and a rock-n-roll Paddy Public Enemy Number One!
So, when I've done my patriotic chore
And burned London to the ground,
I'll head back home to Nenagh
And get pissed every night in town
Like the old folks say, you can't keep a good man down!

# The Fire-Wall

*A brief parting from those dear/ Is the worst [we have] to fear*
~William Yeats, "Under Ben Bulben"

Flames broke the ridge line just the other day,
A day like any other day—I would leap, I would sky-dive,
if I could!
And now the winds whirl screaming
So near to New Years Eve
We would run away, but daren't leave,
For this place is where we need be
If any dead sons, parachutes reversed
Are to raise their voices
From stark caskets, urns and dust
From the iron star's unsleeping rust,
To sing to you, to sing to me,
If any dead hearts
Should beat or burn
If there be any new truth
We might yet learn—
Curious as is any mountain cat—
If any horseman head in hand,
Hand on hat,
Does not pass by, after all, but pauses:
To listen, to speak, to draw near.
To see what new revealing blaze
May vault that silent, smoking wall of fear.

# Under Her Veil In Aurora She Eyes A Rainbow

*May the goddess be just: For the women of Afghanistan and of Iran*
*(He died for the women mujahideen now enslaved—*
*may they see the fiery light of freedom very soon)*

legions withdraw
as legions must
buddhas wrecked
to dust
leaving names
no local tongues quite fit
and the knowing women's voices
silenced
by sharia-thugs—
*litakul alshayatin 'ahsha'ahum fi jahanam*
[Let the devils say their bowels are in hell]
so as the light fades,
as the forward operating base
he died on in Paktia
fades
back into forever
history and
war-mist—
and his comrades sing wan battle- hymns
in Colorado
for him:
"fighting soldiers from the sky"

he perhaps shines
in desert-ice
cloud-rainbows
moon-dogs
north lights
over mountains
we saw
before we thought
of his life
his long love
he may shine
in constellations
only the Afghan women
his warrior sisters
now dare name

*narju 'an takun alualihat saeida*
May the goddess be just

# Within the Silence of the Messengers

*At the birth of each new Era, with a recognizing start . . .*
*Glad Truth's yet mightier man-child yet leaps beneath the Future's heart.*
~from "The Present Crisis" by J.R. Lowell, 1844

Beyond the roar or quiet,
"Behind the dim unknown,"
On the scaffold, in the battle,
In the tomb or birthing room,
We hear only this hush
of wings
barely
stirring the wind—
these angels who sweep around us—
never a word spoken,
never a sword drawn.
For, though their voices be strong,
Though their hearts be brave,
They know that we
would not remember
if they spoke,
could not remember
one
soft word,
nor recall one
fiery blow.
So,
they greet us
in chaste silence,
As we greet them
Only
with ephemeral heart-beats,
as is the way
of our kind
as is the way of
of this:
our unknowing mind.

## Eclipse

A few folks thought
they were going
to heaven today
in the fading light
But they
were disappointed
by the sight
of returning glare
fair is fair

Some say
All went dark
When the bullets hit
his heart
No pain
I tried to see sunrise
For his closed eyes
I tried to see stars
For him
Through his mother's tears
He's in Valhalla
Feasting fighting
loving and laughing
Some soldiers say—
What a happy
pagan warrior's
pay-day!
Some believe in
Whatever it is
that they believe in
Christ
Allah
Odin
Yahweh or Jah, Marx or
Buddha's beggar-bowl,
The stock market, bit coin,
Revolution, evolution,
Or Brigid or Mary's blue robed flow
And yet,

it is
must be
more than they know
and they believe
so
how
could we who lack faith
ever never

know
for sure?
I'd love to say I believe
In something more
I'd love to say he died
Far away
but he
is some
where
near here
today
still
just over the mountain ridge
rainbow cloud
horizon
I'd love to feel
Less
doubtful
about heaven's gauzy veil
The rain falling
But not landing
Dim rainbows fading
The cranes have long ago
Flown away
There are no more
hummingbirds
Here
Since
the eclipse

# Cackle and Scratch

*The Surrendered Voice of Poseur-Identity Poetry
in This Very Real Pandemic*

Listening to a gaggle of urbane, tenured "woke" poets so vain,
(all caucasian by the way),
babble podcast bullshit on sex, gender, correct ways of seeing
in this time of pandemic fear and workers' pain,
hearing them cluck from their chicken-shed perches:
"How can a white male become a human being?"!
One feels impelled to hurl rocks, blaspheme,
ask them if they feel our crude white males are earning humanity
as they go out to work in this
plague time,
while these tame birds cackle and scratch?

But hey politics is so passe, (yawn), anyway.
They have their internal sensitivities, not the dreary boring news.
They get their social sense from the last time, home or away, they
enjoyed being creatively screwed.
Ah, alas, we inhuman white males fail to meet their rarefied
standards of humanity,
of worthiness to sip cocktails, speak rhymes, in their spiritually
evolved presences.
Such fuckery pushes one to the brink!
And then to weep, to know that iron-booted fascism, raw power,
not giving one damn for their poetry slams and pretty prizes,
will cake-walk over this sorry chickenshit land
as our workers die, women men and kids,
human every damned one, white brown black or whatever,
while in their soft cages in Taos, San Fran, London or Manhattan,
such delicate poets of peace and good intentions,
lay their pantoums, villanelles, haiku, sonnets, rotten eggs
for the bosses's pleasure and disdainful laughter

still searching up one another's arses
for their own most appropriate self-identities.
These pullets and plucked hens will compose mournful odes to
the final end
of their sinecures, literary grants,
prizes, perks, podcasts, liberties, and luxuries.

As unions die and workers starve.
White males, white females people of color
All dying together in their humanity.

And then our sweet-tongued versifiers—
damn their lackey eyes—
shall perhaps at last wake up to reminisce
about how they belatedly learned who they really were:
Vile leeches and traitors to the people
who paid their sinecures—
Back when they were free to speak, but squawked.
Back when they could safely talk behind the backs
of the subhuman white males and their families.
As they crouched behind their personas, verse-forms and
masques—sneering at the dumb white
man.
Back before the boot came down, and the real shit hit the fan.

# Widening Gyres

Willie Yeast, ben-bulbing butler
and erstwhile poet of the rising
Could at the very least have arranged
For our second baked coming
to have been sourdough
So
That we might have a wee crunch of bread
Before we're all dead.
So difficult to get good help
These latter days of stimulus payments,
But I guess
you can't always get what you want . . .
while you're slow-rowing
backwards to Byzantium.

# Dien bien phu
*And the Enemy's Crown*

My dad used to tell me tough guy tales
Houdini taking a stomach punch
bayonet drills and Bataan
Senator McCarthy standing up to the Reds
though he'd get quiet
watching Victory at Sea
carriers smoking
kamikaze dives
he shoved a guy upside a wall—

flashed his badge and billy club—
for drunken gibbering at my mom and me
one Stamford street night
He said we had to fight
the Jap enemy
Because of Pearl Harbor
And then
There was Dien Bien Phu
And the Provos blew Lord Mountbatten
Into the sky
My Dad did not like that at all
But I knew why

# A Shadow of Cloud.

Grounded in stiff unbroken REI boots heel-toe
trying to recall that perplexing Easter poem on stone and stream,
humming Christy Moore's song for Seamus Ennis in my brain.
Isleta tribal land to Tome desert Hill through that desolate town
Los Lunas some fourteen miles
—should have stretched the legs before the muscle yelled
near that donut shop on NM 47 headed south the calves yowled
but no "baby-cry," I hobble on
chewing apple-fritter native gift. left bits for birds
dodging noise of old wrecks full of hounds
utterly changed at the fork, I took the ditch road and she the highway—
solo gringo trusting an uncertain crutch—
alpacas moor-hens stunted horses rare old goats ranchers
they called or ran after or stared, enchanted-
reunited, our eyes found stark crosses on the hill
and those mexican kids with vivid faces—
oh! the easter snow so beautiful has faded.
Faded all away.

(Coda:)
She gathered sage along the Hill-side way
And when we returned to level ground,
Tequila and Crown Royal shots all round.
Suffering humanity had been honored this grey day.
Time for well-earned celebration and rejuvenation had been
found. Our sins such as they may be,
had all been swept away, so they say!

*Slainte! ¡Orale!*

## Perhaps Love

perhaps love is ever about mourning, or celebrating,
perhaps both at once, for those of us who live this long
perhaps love is all

# Limbo Rocka

*The bells of hell go ring a ding a ding for you but not for me*

Limbaugh dying shock jock cheers the fools with guns
Demonstrating against social distance
Wants them to get up close and personal with them Liberal bums
Yeah, he'll be dead and rotting
When our people die in millions
Even if the Feds spend trillons
I plan to stay cool, I ain't no damn fool—
I don't want to go down to some redneck asshole's boot
I wanna live long enough to dig up Rush's bones
And piss on them. That would be my blue heaven. Just talking.
To be at a packed Kid Rock show and count the Dead Crackers Walking.

# After All

*Hermosa no es necesariamente buena*
from the epic poem "PTS Me in Time of Isolation"

So this social isolation thing brings time for memories
To emerge—both fond and not so much—
Some even have a tinge of bitter funniness to them
After proper aging they may not be so sad.
(Does blue cheese get better over time or just go bad?)
For instance, today I recall how I left mi Burque barrio—
it was that hot South Valley afternoon
when I was cutting brush
With an electric chainsaw on a long wire
Around the home of a bella bruja I loved
"Midst volumes of literature based on herself"
Who had tied plastic daisies
on the top of her backyard medicinal plants
so as to confuse the hoora's ghetto-birds
and lessen all fear and paranoia among us gente.
(Don't ask. You had to be there.)
Well, as I cut I noticed wee little critters scampering out near my whirling chain
Lotsa legs, black and red hour glasses on them
Yeah, black widows
like in my favorite Country Joe and the Fish Song
"Not So Sweet Martha Lorraine"

*Sweet lady of death wants me to die . . .*

(Inhale, hum along, sing that dead band's song),
I turned off the saw, took a break,
Set myself out back with a bit of home garden grown relaxer.
And made my plan to leave.
Live and let live sez I.

> *The joy of life she dresses in black*
> *With celestial secreta engraved in her back*
> *And her face keeps flashing that she's got the knack,*
> *But you know when you look into her eyes*
> *All she's learned she's had to memorize*
> *And the only way you'll ever get her high*
> *Is to let her do her thing and then watch you die,*
> *Sweet Lorraine, ah, Sweet Lorraine."*

Sometimes discrete retreat is the better part
of it all.
After all.

# Gold Star Dirt, Cash and Glory
*Based on a true American story*

A tough US army commando, battle-tested,
Out of the Army and out of work
With bills to pay and time to kill
Joined up, as may vets did,
with Academi, Erik Prince's merc outfit
(formerly known as Blackwater)
The tough soldier did his job well,
protecting some Mideast interests about which

he could not much tell
when things were very hot in that zone.
But, when things cooled down, Erik Prince's mere outfit
wanted to economize, so they
laid him off and he went home to USA.
Without most of the pay they had said they would pay.
And so that tough commando privately spoke out
About what a rip-off Erik Prince's mercenary business is.
He was not the type of guy to keep the truth from his comrades,
and felt the need to warn them.
Then not long after on an SF training mission overseas
That tough commando got mysteriously shot dead
"By enemy infiltrators" so the Army said.
So the Army said. He got a fancy funeral, fit for a warrior prince,
so the Army said. So the Army said.
Erik Prince? He is not dead. He is rich.
He is Betsy DeVos's brother and he's boosting the Trump demos
in the streets right now, for cold
hard cash.
The traitor son-of-a-bitch.

# Patriot Graves

Let us hold
NO GOLD-STAR-SPANGLED PARTIES
In this sad time
when our heartless President "jokes"
about fake- cures, preens
and publicly jerks himself off
while our beloved people die,
WE MUST MOURN OUR DEAD,
NOT CELEBRATE THESE DEATHS.
I know from harsh personal experience—the Gold Star rag—
that to deflect and deny true mourning of the dead
by declaring "military triumph," saluting the flag,
and calling those dead loved ones loyal "heroes"
is destructive to our selves, to our families
and to our society.
It's the bogus Gold Star propaganda "religion"
that the military uses to keep families quiet, cowed, bribed with
blood money,
so as to deflect any criticism
of the government's callously-wasteful military killing-games—
and keep recruitment going.
While the Sousa bands play on.
In this pandemic, in this time of mass dying,
we do not need more "Gold Star" bogus government
propaganda.
This is not a "war"
in which the Commander in Chief, his Brass and his lackeys
can declare victory, hold parades, salute each other, strike up the
music, send the Blue Angel Jets roaring over us,
and pin medals on themselves.
For having "won."
That bullshit has no place in our public life now.
We need to have days of communal MOURNING
—perhaps each week—
for those who have died tragically in this pandemic.
WE HONOR OUR DEAD BY MOURNING, BY TEARS,
NOT BY MARTIAL DISPLAYS, DRUMS AND BOMBAST.
We honor and remember our sacred dead in their endless silence.

# Lincoln County Road or Armagideon Time
*An American Dive*

The Lamb wept for all sadness to come
Knowing what would be could not never be
Though lions roar and rulers plea.
The people waved palms before their lord, their lamb,
*Kyrie Eleison*
Praying a breeze of peace would vanquish ill winds.
The Lamb smiled in tears, gently touching all minds
Awake to what was to come, embracing their pain, yet
Remembering so the dreaming people could forget.
that sadness tides over you—ebb and flow—
as you touch these dead in mind and heart
they had a dangerous job, they did it well
be proud some say, love them that way
as you recall chant-songs sung in a darkened lodge
around glowing rocks, grandfather stones, bison skull—
earth they say is a warm and loving mother,
we are all still here in her embrace.
yet for all our wishes to believe,
still a sad wave washes, the tide won't turn soon.
somewhere they may only smile
or nowhere they may know nothing
nor care at all
feel not at all

perhaps, love,
perhaps love is ever
about mourning or about celebrating
perhaps both at once,
for those of us who live this long
perhaps, love, perhaps love is all

# A Curse in Time of Mourning, Rage, Angry Love

*Winter in America Blues*

Funny thing now. You can hear time fly by.
Elegiac tones seem to fill quiet mountain air,
As poets pass on and brave workers die
And lovers, fathers are shot down by mercenary scum
in streets of this sad land where cowards carry guns
this spring of our people's blood
this spring of dirty bosses' lies
from this sad spring let flames of righteous summer rise
The next cold winter for America approaches damned fast.
This next winter for America, may it be the bosses' last.
May 6 2020 Indignant Folk Singers of the Pandemapocalypse
Listening to the latest from indignant liberal folk singers—
Folks with lovely voices I like, folks with lyrics meant to make us
deep-think—
Can push one to drink (more) or over the brink—
or even out the door to buy a gun—
Where the hell have all them flowers gone, they wonder—
Did bad man Trump really plow them all under?
On quiet reflection though, and after switching channels, I gotta
say Warren Zevon is
the zinger
among singers in this jagged-edged time
And he's sleeping now—because he's dead
As he said he might be by now
But his back- catalog is deep
And hell I would not be that surprised
If he gave us some ragged new songs soon
Cause like the old folks say,
You really can't keep a good man down
That long—

Check out Life'll Kill Ya and My Shit's Fucked Up
Let us not get sick let us not get scared
Let us not get old and leery
Let us not succumb to pain
Let us not grow old and weary
Grab a hold of that fistful of rain
Ukraine
An incremental scale
Of sanctions useless as Woodrow Wilson's rusty guns.
Interwoven dead trees stript of leaves,
Dried roots entangled, torn.
Rockets' glare. That awful hiss.
"Gas! Gas! Quick!"
The internet's gone down but
That far-off dead poet's blunt
Warning sounds: last century's curse and this.
Lives lost in time, choking, then silent.
Flound'ring in fire, in lime, blind.
The killers lie, as Ukraine dies.
We wonder how high our gas-pump price may rise.
An old man gazes from the precipice, walks away, and sighs.
Russian tank treads clank.

# But You Promised Me Broadway Was Waiting For Me

Y'know, I loved that scene in Far From the Madding Crowd, the movie
Where some young redcoat
buckled and strapped
Ran gallop downhill
afoot
full tilt
At his lady
luv
Slicing closer each time
Nearer
Her
With saber
no doubt
He'd learned
to wield
In redcoat school
And she
Lady-likely
Long hair soft
wafting
Just stood
Pale
There

See, Candy was a Goldwater girl
Catholic finishing school epileptic Republican
Doll faced and longing to bohemian be

So we
Hit the Buffy Sainte Marie village coffee dives
Reelin rockin n die on codeine,
She
Trembling at snakes snails puppy dog tails
Wearing more underwear than I thought legal
And she'd dropped too many of my downs
In my New Rochelle garret
So they pumped her stomach
It had to hurt
And that condescending nun
Trying to see ME through my onyx Dylan shades
Forty years and I dream of beautiful blades
Razor edge fall
Fast and
Close enough to burn
Both her ears

## Safe As Houses
*I feel like I owe it...*
~D. Crosby

Some of us spent our early years flying high
Having fun, switching spouses
While some got down to work and
Made a killing flipping houses.
Fair enough my friends
This was the land of the enterprising free—
Back then—
But after Trump's gang comes back

In twenty twenty five
As the mystics, statistics and CNN say
They well might
We'll need patriots to do what's right
To make those houses safe
For the Maquis carrying on the fight
For the rebels in resistance
Fighting fascist fury in that cold American night.

# Assouf
## *Nomad No More*

The word *assouf,* translates from Tamashek
as "tristesse," or maybe "longing,"
but neither translation quite gets it—
maybe "nostalgia" comes close
but
"the blues" hits the mark—
if played on steel
with a real broken, bloodied bottle-neck—
on the morning after Junior Kimbrough's juke joint
burned
down in Mississippi—
those blues were birthed in Africa, after all,
yet,
you have to have loved the Sahara
for twenty centuries:
its deserts, oases, caravan routes, warriors, women, children and music,
to truly feel *assouf*—
the indigo-draped nomads say
it's "everything that lies beyond the campfire"—
everything we know
and that we cannot know.
How little we knew then,

in our own wandering daze,
when we too were nomad,
of how now we would be nomad
no more—
roaming only in mind in heart,
our bodies static

in a mortgaged land
bought on faith as safe-keep
for our dreams:
a place where those dreams
slowly frayed, dried,
softly died.
It's like when you try so hard
to get home,

and the sun
begins to set,
or it's like when you ride
under stars
in some cool desert night,
and the sun begins
to rise
but
your camel won't stop—
so you nod off,
forgetting fear,

holding to the only song
you still hold
dear:
*NAKID MAHEDJAK YA ASSOUF ERHLALAN?*
What can I do with this eternal longing?
*AWA ISSASMADHEN OULH ERAKHAN?*
What can cool a heart that burns?
That song is *ASSOUF.*

# Afterburner

They roared over, after-burners blazing,
in the middle of a Sangre de Cristo day
when most of us were cutting firewood, watching deer or just lazing.
Wham! Bam! Thank ya, ma'am, our aerial warriors at play!
Some say it's just a training exercise, and we should be glad.
Afghanistan, y'see has mountains like these,
and we're enjoying our safety in the land of the free.
Home of the high- flying brave.
Taliban ain't got no air force, that's for damn sure, Jack.
Raise your eyes to the contrails and whisper the Pledge.
And watch yer back, buddy. Fuckin' hell—Did you serve?
Maybe it's just me,
but low- flying combat planes crashing the air above,
just don't make me feel comfy, y'see.
Too many kids have died. Napalm white phosphorus and bombs,
B52s to raptor drones—the glorious sonic blast of death.

Caskets draped in flags or charred bodies tossed in a ditch.
Does it matter which?
But hey, mate, enjoy your jingo pride.
Shed some patriot tears. Savor the boom. Stick some cotton in both ears.
Crack a few beers.
Put a steak on the grill and smell the burn.

# Dignified Transfer 2013
*Dover Base*

He fell in Afghanistan sometime the day before
The Major from the New Mexico National Guard
couldn't find my house and it was a stormy night in Albuquerque
So we talked by cell phone instead—No dress uniforms at my door—
The Major said it was a clean three shots straight through the heart—
He was dead before he hit the ground and felt no pain, the Major said.
The Major was a father himself he said
I could hear his kid behind the phone and I could hear ice cubes click
I could see my own son reaching up to his dad
The Major called back later and said the government could fly me
to the Dignified Transfer at Dover base
I asked where that was and the Major said he thought it was

"Maybe in Indianapolis . . .," but he wasn't sure exactly where it was.

I looked it up on Google and found it is at Dover Delaware
Far from New Mexico. Far from here.
And the Major and his Army never did get me there.
After all.

I don't know where my son is
I know he is beautiful there.

# Buy Me a Ticket to Ride
*for Gurf Morlix and Blaze Foley*

Dreamt some joker called me a Messiah,
And I mighta cleaned his clock, y'all,
But I was duct- taped in my coffin,
Waiting to ride that hound in
To heaven for free.
To find my satisfied mind
But first, them angels say,
If I want to meet John Prine
I have to not bitch or whine
And just proof- read
My whole memoir-biography
Called "Blaze Gone to Glory"—
It's ten million pages long,

Single spaced yellow- pad scrawl
Stuck up on my inside box- lid wall!
But, it would make
One hell of a song, y'all
So I'll sing it to that pretty lady
With two or three kids
Waiting patiently beside me.
She don't seem to mind
My Arkansas hillbilly drawl
And we both have all the sweet time
In this weary old world
To kill.

# Heartbreak Ridge

his mom back east just sighed another poor boy off to fight the
rich man's war
and I crouch in a desert learning to read in the dark: Joseph
Conrad and Adrienne Rich
Dylan's masters of war rotating with Joe Strummer's version of
Tom Moore's "Minstrel Boy"

but he is so far far away and now

HOME

is just a four letter word . . .

we send our stories out anyway: painted trains roll rickety clack
north on Santa Fe track,

box-car greetings in spray-paint color cross the Indian lands,

barrio words bound for Colorado glory
while the dear prez is on the radio,
droning out his story

spray-can work on North Philly streets was art-crimes for the kid
who wrote and ran,

best writer his English teacher ever read, she said,

who turned his tales in late,

too busy sharking pool, fight-clubbin', dodging cops, too cool for
school
who took his diploma late anyway and didn't get to walk the aisle,
but rode off instead in that damned recruiter's car,
to Basic where he shaved his tuff guy chin growth

and was taught salute march fight

and how to mow down trees with the Army's grand Squad
Automatic Weapon SAW

like in that GI picture postcard he mailed home
and jump from planes when the word was JUMP

though he hated it

and lead his guys when the word WAR got real
like it did for his grand-dad in the forties
and for all those battle-stock men back up the family line,
heroes or mercenaries true to tradition
and that Minstrel Boy song to the war has gone
his fathers' swords girded on— Wild Geese, brave Harp!
the history books tell us they tell us so well
how FDR put poor folks' art in public display WPA,
and respectable if tinged by Eleanor's democratic light red hue—

then Pearl Harbor blew

and Woody strummed his fascist-slaying six-stringed axe

and sailed the rough seas singing
"Ruben James—tell me what were their names?"
and took torpedo hits on every craft he shipped on

which was no joke
yet roared out word of our fighting kids
and said what must be said
about this land and which side we're on,
and those were glory days indeed:
the good fight could be good
and then we had peace . . .
of a sort . . .
and then . . .

The Towers of New York dropped—
no Flava Flav joke in your town
nine one one— his birthday back in 1981—

"no woman no cry"—

so, twenty years on with his hippy-rasta hair shorn
and the same Pentagon blown that

we so far far back in our own late child-time danced before and
tried to lift off the ground

in spirit smoke sex and laughter exorcism-levitation
with our flowered tresses flowing
and Tuli Kuperferberg that grand mensch chanting

OUT DEMONS OUT—

and Norman Mailer gulping bourbon paddy-wagoned
facing down a bellicose American Nazi while we grasped for
words to spell it out:

NO . . . MORE . . . WAR—

as armies in the night we had to put away childish things,

right?

This new fight he's in just might be just and right
for all the snake-oil crap and flag-wrapped lies—

it could well be wrong that same sad old song sung by bad men
whose sons eat cake

who send the hard and best of our young

to mountains where the empire's legions feared to tread and poor
squaddies bled

as Kipling said

and the brave comrades in Red also were shot dead with bullets
we sent to warriors of God
yet our young still go, though donkey trains balk on those
heartbreaking ridges—

and black-hawks come down filled with heroes:
early death tumbling from above—

still soldiers don't ask about all that soldiers are asked to do and
soldiers just do what soldiers

must do

do what we must do: what we need to do is what they need us to
do

just do it till this is done—send love

send postcards send toothpaste hard candy send jokes pictures of
beauty

send body armor send pride send words send love—
he sends back email short bursts yahoo love to mom and his girl
flame tenders who find in their hearts' eyes snapshots from that
awful Asian ridge

wipe the tears see the sights
the sites
through night-scope sights:
starlight starbright first star you see tonight
is where our prayers light that ridge, shine bright
bring our boys, our girls home, man
when this war ends this war ends this war ends

the word will be

revolution of those words now spinning in his head

sir yes sir yes ma'am yes but

will they all still give a damn? tumbling off that ridge, tumbling over and over—

will he send us letters
X? or Y? or Z?
Now maybe

We'll chant AUM with sweet gone old AG—and know the best minds of this generation are

angry and taught to be, damned well ought to be!

Word

Coming back home soon
Soon come home soon
Word
Love word home
HOME!
Sweet sweet home.

## Lá an Dreoilín
## (how Them hungry Birds Flew)

Even Saint Stephen might have had to admit
Life can be pointless and transient,
As must it be for them treacherous wrens
Or those too- patient island folk.
Yet some say we should act as if
Existence could be beautiful itself
Like a robin's call or a quick, clean death--
If such epiphanies exist
At all,
like, for instance,
the cries of laughing gulls
over
Bikini Atoll.

# how They Do So Plan for Us

He my son
"lived in honor"
they say
died in war
correctly
they tell me—
that high commandant of NATO and National Guard Generals
and the Spec Ops brotherhood
all with one stern voice say:
he was a hero (meaning he is alright in hero-land Valhalla-heaven
or simply in the hearts of living comrades all trained to love him
well
—I needn't fret behind my Gold Star pin,
i am advised to take comfort and warmth as loyal parents do

Now, to them,
He is nearly a Myth
Who fell to fire
Loyally
for them and for our beloved families
and for their well considered battle plans
and border walls
Far over there
somewhere
wherever they say it was
where no one here
really
knows where
and they tell me
he died for freedom for peace in defense of our dear land
and people
for honor
against terror and cowardice,
fear
and savage flames.

As the nuke nations rattle their unimaginable firestorm spears,
threatening to bring liquids of human bodies bubbling on a
concrete floor,
let us draw a veil.
Let us ignore the fascist dog-babble for a while.

Here,
I am walking and reading mysterious irish poems of thomas
kinsella
feeling heartbeats in cool cloudy river air.
I am happy to be here;
I think my son is with me, happy as well
to be here.
We feel no fear.

In this fog of peace,as they say,
I walk along a shallow river ocean
while women work far ashore
each pressing her earnest soul
against that grinding wheel of death,
each railing in her quiet voice at the inevitability of war,
of daughters sons mothers and fathers
dying
of children dead
of tidal dread.

Come round at last here in even this dry land of sun
contemplating how it will be to be . . . to be old,
very old,

contemplating that holy cold,
imagining the calculations over Ukraine or Iraq
over Russia
over Pakistan Aghanistan India Vietnam
over China over China over China
over Palestine
over Africa
over all borders
over all revolutions begun and crushed
and the arithmetic of bones involved.

Then,
shuddering awake and seeing myself some fine old poet,
strolling here in Albuquerque late winter
on the border of mad and wise
on the border of USA and world
and realizing with a startle that I am now returned to myself,
in joy, smiling as my son,very much here in this borderland,
laughs.
"Old man old man,"
he sings to his crazy old man,
we each in our myths mad,
and sane joyous brave and wild.

oh
I weep happily for my
sweet dead child.
and, oh, i laugh
in joy at long long last
for the borders crossed
for the lands freed
for the liberating fire this time
for the flames

# Worlds Open on Smokey Worlds

*"Have you news of my boy Jack?"*
*Not this tide.*
*"When d'you think that he'll come back?"*
*Not with this wind blowing, and this tide.*
~Rudyard Kipling, *My Boy Jack*

that sadness tides over you
as you touch the dead
in mind and heart
he had a dangerous job
he did it well
be proud some say
love him that way
as you recall the chant
their songs sung
before their glowing rocks
grandfather stones
mother earth they say
is warm and loving
we are all still here
yet for all your wishes to believe
that sad wave washes
the tide won't turn soon
somewhere he may only smile
or nowhere he may know
nothing at all care not at all

# TAKE AWAY

Light ricochet
off last late leaves
far off bugling elk
mountain high October dying
warmer than you'd think
with snow on the ridge
Boots crunch past
A silent stone cairn
I don't know much
of thought just feel
But an art-maker says
There's a sphere here
Hid in the refractive bend
of time
Near end, fully begun
Again:
When slugs knocked
light and sight
out
Did his heart know
It wasn't over?

## I do

This mountain morning
as I think of the fallen heroes
of Spain
of Gardez Base
of this falling rising world
May you fall softy
rise gently
in our holy star's blaze
in our fierce moon's pull

# St Magdelene

*Dearly Beloved...*
~Romans 12:19

Saint Magdelene
One black rose
adorns her still body
He bends to cleanse her wounds with his own long hair
as she once cleansed his, prepares to craft her coffin,
drive nails gently home.
This Easter Monday night, hard angels shiver in that gunman's cold shadow,
as her warm blood, darkening, soaks this War Zone pavement,
touching the throw-down dropped beside her corpse.
Her killer preps his story, wipes clean his lapel camera, calls in his chits,
as the risen Christ sheds lagrimas de sangre
for love, law and innocence lost, for unholy murder in these dirty streets of Alburquerque .

# Buddha's Wagon

*Sex and the Car Bomb, Marching Forth 2021*
(with apologies to singer Neal Young)

Ashli Babbit was a Dead head. Now she's just dead.
Poor Ashli, Air Force Vet, bankrupt nuke- plant slave,
Would-be soldier of Cowboy's 4 Trump's True -Q Crew
Had a cowboy problem she never really knew
That January 6 afternoon in DC, y'see.
She rode bare-back a mad stallion of delusion
That whispered, "Babe, The Storm is near!"
But there's nothing a Patriot need fear,
So she plunged through a shattered US Capitol window
Chasing her dark dream towards some mirage of light
To her harsh black-out end- of- life. To find what she sought.
As bloated Daddy Trump gloated at what his words had wrought.
"Don't tread on me," hissed snake- flags flown then and now.
And what if you did know her and found her dead on the floor,
A bloody Trump Flag draped over her, looking her final best,
A cop's 40- caliber slug through her chest?
Would you mourn? Would you kneel and pray for her soul?
Or might you just load up a pickup with fertilizer, like bomber- martyr McVeigh,
Or like car-bomber, Mario Buda, whose Wall Street dynamite- wagon slew so
many, a century ago—
Take off your mask, and holler, "Okay boys, let's roll! As go one, so go all."
As you hum some horrid Horst Wessel marching song.
Hitler's ghost, cowboyed- up like Rowdy Yates on Wagon Train,
Stetson cocked on his head, rebel flag and big gun in hand,
Rolling down that road to Santa Fe or Washington DC,
A seditious Siddhartha seeking to Buda be,
Seeking satori in blood and fire,
Lusting, dear Lord, for you to kill him
Not with a flood this time, but with fire.
And sweet Jesus, if you only knew:
It will feel like horse-shit, scraped off your shoe.

# hirschman
*A Poem in Three Parts*

I.
Caro Jack in the Morning of this New World
*Don't mourn. Organize.*

Jack Hirschman in the City Lights stacks declaiming his Arcanes
Where Sharon Doubiago first introduced us years ago
Jack on the bus riding to a reading red scarf wrapped
Smiling with his satchel of poems under his arm
Jack singing in Russian to the good woman of Spec's
Who gave him a chocolate cake and a hug for his birthday
Jack at the Buddhist school teaching the Naropa kids

The Manifesto greatest poem of all,
As Allen's double rainbow graced the Boulder sky!
Jack coming home after an evening of people's poetry work
To Aggie and we two visitors from afar
Filling our glasses with vodka or wine
Then reciting "Sailing to Byzantium" in its entirety
From memory to show us what pure poetry can mean
To show us what the mind can be to show the red- way
As revolution rose from the streets of North Beach
As Jack laughed and loved and danced and sang
As our lives rolled on as the world began
As Jack lives with us each brave new dawn

II.
Jack in the Long March

Most poets are like meteors slicing our sky
They flash, are beautiful and then are gone in the blink of an eye.
Into the endless black.
Most poets, even fine and lovely ones, will be forgotten
In the long run. Most poets are not poets like Jack.
History will not forget Jack Hirschman.
Viva Jack Hirschman. Blazing bright. *¡Siempre!*
Jack Hirschman. *¡Presente!*

III.
Jack, Manifest

"Let the ruling classes tremble at a Communistic revolution. The proletarians have nothing to lose but
their chains. They have a world to win.
Workers of all countries unite!"
*Mira, Compa* Jack. *¡Venceremos!*

# Sonny Rollins

*There is no endgame in music. . . . That's why I keep practicing*
~S.R., 2007 interview
*There is a crack, a crack in everything.*
*That's how the light gets in.*
~Leonard Cohen

on stage, dressed sharp
sacred sax singing
that song
came down
through *Colossus*
through silence
through Basie
n
Trane,
through Miles
through Buddha's smile
n
Bessie Smith's graveyard dream
through all those
soft standards
that carried scared hearts
through good wars
that weren't so good
in the end
came down through
all the dirty crap
they sell
to distract
to tear
your eyes
your ears
from real
you never
bought
their shit,

*maestro*
even up in the sticks
where you fled
their poison
one holy September
morning
full of joy
before all the sky
before all the sky
opened
as if fear
really
did
not
matter
as
brave and lonely as
when
you stood wild
practicing
your cry
on Williamsburg Bridge
for Brooklyn
for Manhattan
for the millions more to come
or
blowing only
for *you*
and only
for every ear
ever
opened
anywhere
how near
we are
how near

# Jerry Garcia Done Gone Long Gone

*The winds of fate blow where they will,*
*I'll give you three Al Purdys for a Twenty dollar bill!*
~Bruce Cockburn from his album "Bone On Bone"

I'm so Sick of the Sixties,
Smoky nostalgia's a bore
Teach Your Children Well—Hell!
It's Germany 1934.
So Sing Me No More
Fish- Cheery Imagine There's No War Songs
(Woodstock Was a Mud n Granola Fiddle-Fun Fest
While Indochina Burned)
Billy Strings doing War Pigs
Is just about all I can take
Now that the Ramones and Strummer
are gone
I don't want to hear old man Neil sing about
Her dead on the ground
When the National Guard is coming round
Again
He didn't know her
And who is she, anyway to him
But a sentimental hook for a hit song
To help with the payments on his ranch?
Young Neil nor Joni never got gassed, shot or beat- up
And no cop knocked the silver spoon
Out of any Canadian folkie's dulcet mouth
And I don't give a damn about Virgil Kane's
See-shesh brother buried down south
I don't want to hear Joanie wailing
Kumbaya mi lawd
Cause she thinks Zimmy or her daddy did her wrong
So long, long ago
Shucks!

She made her bucks
I don't want to ever again hear Slick Gracie
Howl about weatherwoman Diana
Building a bomb to kill SDS
While her Starship Plane cruises first class
In comfy Owsley retirement dreams
I don't want to hear you whine
Against being so rich and so outta touch
with the times Watchman Tom and your rusty rage machine
And
Goddesses save us from Septuagenarian Springsteen!
And hey Bob your neighborhood bully's
Crossed the line, man, for real this time.
How does it feel? To be a pawn in their game?
The Glimmer Twins are now just faded junkies
Not street fighting rebels
Or sexy dancing monkeys
So
Sing us no more vain peace freak battle- songs
As the Empire roars
You dying Nero-dinosaurs
Get your tired candy asses in gear
Or get your slimey hippy ear-worms outta my ear
Lou Reed said it best, and Lou is long long gone:
March of the wooden soldiers
All you protest kids:
White Light! White Heat!
I say . . . tin soldiers and Trump and J.D. Vance are coming.
Yer finally on yer own.
Fahgettaboutit! Reetpapareet!
Just play me Martha & the Vandellas doing "Dancing in the Street

# Aiséirí
## "Resurrection in English"
### (After Emily Dickinson, perhaps)

Fall, lightly, to that blue light
This poem is not me
This flight may be fancy
But never worry
If we fall
Don't fret—this text is not you, either.
We can fly free in this song
Whomever we may be.
This go-round, forget your parachute.
*Trust your cape.*[1]
It's like that eerie December concert
When Miles Davis turned his back on us
But held one delicious aching note
For what seemed all night long
Then he left the stage: *Ite, Missa est!*
And we silently filed out
Into the bleak Massachusetts night.
Michelangelo's roman steps descend
Like a river without end
Yet, Rainier Rilke, from his deep-diving heart,
Reminds us that *everything serious is difficult.*
Yet, were it easy to find solitude together,
As easy perhaps as sex can be,
Or were it as easy as it is to fall backwards
Into a rushing mountain stream,
Then we might tumble laughing
Past rapids, round fierce rocks,
Until we dream- drift at last
No more asking why
Out to that moon-tugged rolling sea.
Up towards that azure endless sky

---

[1] Guy Clark, "Always Trust Your Cape"

# Brush/fire

So when those flames flare
all electric lights out—
how do gentle poets
brush their teeth, their tresses,
in char, in radioactive dark?

# White Castle is a Very Good Place

Gloria told me her story for an hour or more
on a stoop in Gentilly
just outside the racetrack
that first Jazz Fest weekend after the Thing That Happened:
They pointed guns at us bigger than me on the end of that bridge
so we turned back
and we had to get
off that bridge anyway
but we all kept walking to find help
and people coming back the other way towards us
said don't go to the Superbowl
its bad there
so we did not
and we found somebody's car that still ran
and started towards Baton Rouge
but people at a gas stop
told us they didn't want us up there
and we wouldn't be welcomed
that far up the river
probably because of the crazy stuff
some people did
barbecuing and drinking and guns and all that
that they heard about on the tv
so we stopped in White Castle, Louisiana,
and they are good people there
and they helped us
and they said I was the queen
and my husband was the king
he's seventy- six and I'm seventy- one now
and we didn't believe the water would rise so high
but it surely did

# Waiting for the Hog Farm to Serve Breakfast?

It's twenty twenty-four as Fall chill
rolls in.
And this ain't the summer of love!
The crazy, rich,
old white lady
who left her mind at Woodstock '69.
with her volumes of rockstar snapshots
based on herself
like sweet Loraine
wheels
her paisley-dotted hippy-happy-times bus
around Santa Fe,
blaring dead Kennedy campaign songs
and Country Joe's hits
like "Super Bird"
and Randy Newman's "Rednecks"
—without any hint of irony.
From those hyped-up speakers
she paid so dearly for—
"JOIN US," she shrieks—
We are MAGA and MAHA, we will save you
and feed you granola, too.
We have the Holy Word straight up from Q!"
She leaps about laughing like a sated vampire
on Owsley's best bloody brew,
dreaming of peace and all the love
she knew—hey,
they shot Johnny Lennon, and George Wallace, too,
while those "bomber-death planes"
raped Vietnam—
Meanwhile, as Colbert smirks,

on the front lines
of the real world
the guns go off
and children fall
and teachers fall
and the bombs fall
on Gaza
and the poor hold on
as best they may
and in saner countries
far away
the worried people
say
What if Trump wins?
What if?
But,
we do what we can do.
We do.
It's true.
Remember, will you,
that
at least
we tried?

# The Brink (Someday We'll Ride Again)
### (Perhaps a song, after Michael McClure)

All ye beloved souls gone rogue,
ye wan jumpers
from Taos Gorge Bridge,
steel pier,
North Tower 84th floor
a C130 Super Hercules door
the jagged doors of perception
or any tempting edge
Far or near—
to hell with fetters and fear!
Moonshine blind, what other kind
of vision would you choose, cousins?
Over the edge, canyon deep,
to the land of sleep,
leap and dream,
leap and dream!
If you must come over, lonely rovers,
trust your hero's capes:
May you ever
fall as you fly,
fly as you fall.
What can we say
this sad old day?
We'll so miss you,
miss you, that's all.
Moonshine blind, what other kind
of quest would be best, wanderers?
You on your winged beast
and me on my rocker,
or off,

yet at least
should we choose
win or lose
to hang tough or leap
down from the edge, to some land of safe-keep?
Reap as you sow, sow as you reap.
Leap and sleep, reap and dream.
Laugh as you laughed, lovely rovers!
Love as we loved you, forever.
Fall as you fly, like a feather.
We'll miss you,
miss you,
miss you, all.
Fall Softly,
Wild Rover,
If You Must
Tumble
Over.

# Cyberia

*For the Commissars of Poetry*

I dreamt I was Comrade Yevtushenko dodging or schmoozing the KGB
I dreamed that I joined the State Poetry Society:
Meetings every Tuesday with cold old pizza, borscht and Schlitz
While they defined rhyme schemes, I got the shits
They cut my wrists and sucked real hard
And then they sent me a membership card
*Yer one of us now, lad, blood in blood out!*
*We love you and your pantoums! Of that there's no doubt!*
It was better than the Gulag, I guess,
But then, *tovarichi*, it got much worse.
I dreamt I was Mayakovsky and the Versifiers Soviet Guild caught me
Made me pay dues to spit out true anti-capitalist ML poetry:
So I composed a sonnet about Allen Ginsberg's shoe,
Illegal mezcal, glasnost and Gorbachev's tattoo.
Then the dream ended of a sudden, and I dozed off anew—
Slept so well, friends, I woke up wrapped in an ice-blue haiku.

> *So mnoyu vot chto proiskhodit*
> "That's what is happening to me"

# Boogaloo
*Quid agis hodie?*
(meet you after Carlow)

Blood on the street here,
Where once you stood.
Smells like . . . victory!
Ah, hate does feel fine,
It's why all them fascist religions
Do make us feel so GOOD,
Why battle-songs rhyme.
We feel so strong for one another.
Another morning it could be love.
Black banners afloat, visor down,
Up with halberd out with sword
On we go. My lord!
But it's just for a time.
Until that awful morning AFTER.
After the gore is scattered,
After the fight's won, or lost
Let us now count up the cost.
Skulls and ribcages glisten in morning frost
Dear my beloved what was it you said?
Please don't bury me down in that cold old ground.
You see I still want to be alive. I want to stay around.
I was never fonder of you.
Enemy, my love.

Now that's fair play to you, trying to recall what it WAS.
To hear your mother pray. To see another sunrise day.
Rise.
Mother spoke only Latin all her live long days.
*Quid agis hodie?*
Today when there are no more todays.
When the world is but haze.
When we meet again some midnight darkened date.
Nice to meet you finally after all the mindless hate
What the bloody hell do you have to say to me?
And in which dead language will that be?

# Calavera Sunsets: All Remind Me of That

*Too long a sacrifice can make a stone of the heart,*
that sage Irish poet said of his dead, friend and foe,
who fell in 1916 honor beneath the rebel flag of Starry Plow
in a war otherwise forgotten by many now.
I've long been a reader of wise old words.
Decades later, trying not to shatter,
I did read old battle-poems for odd, wary solace,
*for peace comes dropping slow* sang the haughty Irish bard,
and my minstrel-boy has gone to war for so long.
 Then I did read those formal condolences
which trickle in from his Command,
General Breedlove, the Prez, and that lot,
starry American war-guidons above each letterhead:
*Rest assured, Sir, you are in our thoughts.*
Yet for a month then as I wrote these lines—
but seven years now here in Coronavirus times—
he has been dead: *changed utterly* as old man Yeats said.
Folded flags, Purple Hearts, Green Beret, dog tags
and his childhood snapshots all remind me of that.
For thirty- two grand years he was alive:
his laughter, his smile and his emails from Afghanistan—
*I'll be home soon, old man, love, Liam* all remind me of that.
So we old poets heal, dancing with skull-faced rebel women—
terrible beauties for fair, Willie boyo, gone gone Maudies all—
in clear South Valley Albuquerque air,
in Marigold- Sunset blaze of this Sunday of the Beloved Dead.
When all holy red sun banners had finally set,
and the dark came to wrap our mortal souls,

I beat loud wild taps on my Irish skin-drum
outside some curandera- poet's Atrisco gate,
asking only for prayers for my son,
asking only for peace to soften breaking hearts,
as we face down the horror of his death
yet celebrate the joy of his life
laughing through tears behind my fierce gabacho Calavera paint
within a ceremony of sacred magic mushroom aura
deep here within this heart
and yes I know that candles burned
and Spanish prayers were said
and yes at peace we are, he and I
these years of slow dropping peace
these years of war that ended long ago

## Canción

*Gringo Grito O Gabacho Sueno de Burque*
for Keith Sanchez y Stoic Frame—
Homies Till the Wheels Fall Off

The iguana who winks, the old man who thinks:
Peeling green chiles, stringing ristras of red
Never talk to "la jura,"
Say your prayers before bed.
Celebrate San Patricio and Santana's guitar
Wend this road many years on
Whistling gypsy rover over the hill
Know there'll be no Spanish goodbye song

*Caminamos a través de nosotros mismos,*
*Pero siempre encontrándonos con nosotros mismos.*
*(Chorus:)Panza llena corazon contenta,*
*Gracias a dios y la Buena cocinera!*

I remember those tears, those strolls by the rio
*Con setas mágicas,*
Those laughs—*¡Ay, dios mios!*
Those South Valley sunsets, dark eyes, your grito so wild,
Waking to rooster crows, your smile and your question,
"Scrambled or juicy, Viejo?" Always "Christmas" my reply.
The ghetto birds buzzing, cops overseeing your crops,
Bullets tapping down on tin roofs rattle tat a tat,
Of a New Years Eve, Cinqo or Fourth of July.

*!Panza llena corazon contenta,*
*Gracias a dios y la Buena cocinera!*

Black widows lurking, pitbulls lunging, Penitentes chant,
Tequila shots, weddings, Good Friday pilgrims climb Tome Hill,
Mad dog stares, black berets, smokey mota,
Flaunted bling, hidden guns, enchiladas and bad chiva.

*!Panza llena corazon contenta,
Gracias a dios y la Buena cocinera!*

Slinging hay bales, breathing soft through warrior sweats,
And failing to learn how to make adobe bricks
Funerals and limpias, the healing light.
The curandera's poetry, mad as midnight.And candles lit for the newly dead, the ancient dead.
The prayers that were said as all prayers must be said.

*!Panza llena corazon contenta,
Gracias a dios y la Buena cocinera!*

All bad, huh?

# A Gentile Kaddish Sung for All Fallen in the Sun

No, son, only a lucky few of us are Jews—
thick micks, Belgians, Germans—
we were and are—yet proud enough to have known those earth
deep people of that Tribe of Moses, or the Gente of Nuevo
Mexico and the loving folk of Vietnam Louisiane, Africa, Spain—
oh, any fine land where they still breathe free Afghanistan Iraq
those of faith those of Allah or even the good believers in Pope
or Lenin, Rastafari or Buddha, for sweet Christ's sake!
even those who cherish this Fourth
this weird old falling down
Amerikay
Hey!
brother
son
strong fighter
man
I, non-Jew old man
of yours
yet do strive to sing
Kaddish
for you
in this troubled land
in
anyway I can
I do
This mountain morning
as I think of the fallen heroes
of Spain
of Gardez Base
of this falling rising world
May you fall softy
rise gently
in our holy star's blaze
in our fierce moon's pull

# This Bleak Sadness

*For Mosab Abu Toha*

This bleak sadness brings with its acceptance
 the question of disappointment,
the question of how long,
The wonder of how life feels, how life fails,
As the Israelis do murder in Gaza.
As the poets squabble over awards, money
Grants and recognition, placement on the page,
As the Israelis do murder in Gaza.
An American poet says he is just not in the mood
For unpleasantness or mischief,
These latter days of thanks,
These days of bombs and tanks
As the Israelis do murder in Gaza.
A Palestinian poet tells of his seven- year- old niece
Who died when the Israelis did murder in Gaza:
Her smiling picture lights his cell phone
As the Israelis do murder in Gaza.
And when will the sadness end
When will the rain of poems in blood desist?
When oh when
When will the Israelis cease their murder,
In Gaza?

## Coot Vicious in Memory
*For Bob Warren*

He took that email handle half in jest, half in dead seriousness.
He was old enough to raise a righteous fist if he must.
He was young enough to call out the phony, the unjust.
Like John Brown, bearded and fierce,
He held his Bible in one hand, dear brother
An avenging sword, good sister, in the other.
He would not dance your minuet nor force a sonnet or fol de roll de roll,
A pantoum or villanelle seemed to him pretentious as hell.
Yet his litanies, adopted or not, burn like curses, like prayers
You would not want to meet him in the Valencia County dark
Yet he brought light anywhere in this wide world he went—
Deep into Detroit, Texas, Burque, Los Lunas, your open heart—
And a laugh
And a warning fresh and stern.
Here's the damn good news:
Take the gospel seriously ye Christians
Or face the wrath of conscience
Of a Son of Man risen in fury
To confront ye
With a 357 mag or a taught line of poesie.
Take his name in vain,
At your peril.
Forget him not, comrades
He walked the earth like ye and me.
He watches. Have no fear.
Bring the next fiery wave.
Souls were born to save.

# oh omar in darkness, what the hell ya dreaming now?

in that night we dreamed
as you could well dream
macho mateen destroyer of worlds
of what could have been, of what could be—why not turn those
bullets away—with love and poetry and songs and laughter—and
touch and kisses—so they spin off into the sea of false
memory—and fade away like ice melting in warm waters—of our
heart-blood while our brothers sisters lovers and friends—all
alive—all fresh and wild—arise—open their eyes—recognize
us—even you—poor little omar looking for love, habibi, and
smile? Hey! we were only dreaming—such a bad joke,
hermano—now, here we are together forever let's dance even
you, oh flatfoot clumsy pendejo omar! drop your gun, brother
fool, take our hands and dance then the sun arose once more and
we whirled as we all turned to light, turned to love

# No Nuke is tactical

*A spectre haunting: for China Mieville*

"Mayday Mayday Mayday!"
Vinegar Hill—
Stark cross or Starry Plough,
Waving scythes against grapeshot.
NATO's catspaw or Mother Russia's last chance.
Incense and poison gas.
Rebels crouch in shadow
Or curse the fallen church, yet
All climb to self- crucifixion.
Martyrs tumble, mountains rumble:
Wasted blood,
Wasted time.
Four cups of wine or
A *Limpia* with medicines of angels:
Children's laughter, sweet and gorey.
Hoist prayers in smoke and glory!
Don your red sash and dance!
Dance!
The unrattling snake still strikes!
*Allahumma Ameen!*
Bring the empire down
Pass the bottle round!
Dot dot dot
Dash dash dash
Dot dot dot
■■■ ▬▬ ▬▬ ▬▬ ■■■
"Breach is Breach!"
And no nuke launched will be tactical.

# A Well Regulated Militia
*for Carolyn Chute*

We'd been well out
of New York
three years by then
our own kid walking free under
cool stars and aurora borealis
on the odd nights
but
Tonight it was
just
more
Moonlight in Vermont
and
ragged Bob Sweet
seventh generation
Green Mountain Boy
ditch digger and purported bigamist
illiterate but armed
and crookedly smiling
knocked on our hippy cabin door

because
he had
shot that doe
dead in her face
way out of season
and needed help
so
me and him
lugged her
the long way
over that ridge
where wardens never went

alone
Bob leaning on his
old rifle
like it was
a walking stick
and who knew if
it was
loaded?
to Bob's rugged shack

way back

where dogs howled kids wailed
for yellow cheese and Lays
potato chips
coca cola Little Debbies cakes

and

Bob's rough old lady popped 'ludes
and bitched
and there was a mess of
kitchen knives,
busted glass,
cheap beer
and The Dukes of Hazard was
on the tube
and it took longer than I hoped

yet
still
for all
that mess
and all that confusion
blood
and unheard prayers
a slow simmered deer meat stew

on a cold
back hollow
moon charmed
night
coupla shots
of ginger brandy
leeks and potatoes in the pot
Charlie Pride
on the box
did
taste
so
damned
fine

# Shane MacGowan in the Green Room, 1987

*Oh the wind that blows to the north and south*
*it blows to the east and west*

It's like that ragged old guy in a tube station
coulda been a fookin hero in the Spanish Civil War
risked his damn life for the people
how the hell
do we know?
and he's just some crumbled up bearded geezer now
for all the punk kids to have a laugh about
who
don't even know
what the fookin Spanish Civil War was anyway
what the hell
Cuchulainn on his sickbed
having a drink
in the morning
one last go
in a brothel in Madrid
or
trapped
with Frank Ryan in Germany
listening to the rattle
of death trains
and nothing can be done about it
at all
at all
but get up and roar
his poor
fookin heart out
and thats all he can do
in'it?

then Shane laughed that sneezing laugh
took one more swig
of Maalox
with his left
gulp of Guinness
with his right
doctor told me
stay off
the fookin whiskey
for a while
he fookin did
the right
old
fookin
bastard
that
he is

# Lock Up & Get Out

(Prepping for Project 2025)
*Freddy Get Ready, Rock Steady!*
~Warren Zevon, "Johnny Strikes Up the Band"

Get locked up!
Even if only for a night
Cause you insulted a cop
Or asked the cops to let you in
Even if you just visit a cell
For an hour or two or three
On some pretext of being
A journalist, a poet, a religious zealot
An architect, a lawyer, a drunk, an illegal immigrant, a refugee,
A person of color, a commie or a lib or queer —
Just figure out how to get in
You're smart enough to do that,
And then when you are in
Think about how it would feel
Not to be able to get out
And feel that feeling.
It's real.
Now you are ready to support
The Resistance. Try to stay free.
Cause that's where it's gonna be.

# Kabul Sunset

*Mourn Your Dead Now,*
*Land of the Free*

(As proud-robed mujahideen
Give wary thanks in bearded faces
To Allah in the ruins
Of Forward Operating Bases
Daubed in sad skull-graffiti boasts
Of long-departed Yanks
In shadows of rusting Russian tanks.)

coII have heard or read wise poignant words.
They've sewn together my shifting drifting worlds.
Kipling, Shakespeare, John Prine, James Wright,
Lennon, Dylan, whatever gets me through the night
Larry Kirwan's "Fallujah" song or Patrick Sky,
Diving into the wreck of the Iliad, the Tain,
With sweet Ocean Vuong or some haughty Irish bard
Hoping not to shatter,
I read old battle-poems for wary solace:
My own true minstrel-boy gone to war for so long.
Star-flecked American war-guidons above each letterhead:
"Rest assured, Sir, you are in our thoughts."
I watched the Albuquerque sun rise
For him, as I feared he had no eyes.
That awful morning long ago.
I was a foolish dad, for he saw, I know.
Went mad a month then as I first wrote frantic lines —
"Dover Base" and other cries,
Bitter sighs. I knew he was dead.
We've gone years now to these Coronavirus times —
"changed utterly" as old Yeats said.
Do old poets ever heal, as nations move on?
In Marigold-Sunset blaze of Sunday of the Beloved Dead.
When all holy red sun banners had finally set,
and the dark came to wrap our mortal souls,
Spanish prayers were said
and yes at peace we are, he and I
these many years of peace dropping slow
these years of a war that should have ended long ago

# Enough

*For Jeannie, of course*

Stroll these woods, hear thrushes sing,
Woodpeckers hammer trunks, hummingbirds buzz,
See hungry hawks swoop, vultures soar, bats swoop
Where bears shove stones aside, elk tramp out trails and poop,
Mule deer graze right to our cabin porch unafraid.
Coyotes lurk, bobcats lurch—cougars we never see prowl.
Where you and I also unafraid
Meet eyes hold hands
Hug in the morning sunrise light feed the pups
Where we laugh, hug, smile, even weep,
One hopes with our loving energy being enough . . .
To keep the sun rising, the flowers waving
the colors shifting, clouds over ridge, and then the stars firing up—
so, we and all these critters may sleep,
safe not afraid of anything at all.
Not any thing at all.

# Acknowledgements

Several of these poems have appeared in
    *Malpais Review*
    *Best American Poetry*
    *New York Quarterly*
    *Revista Literaria Monolito*
    *Fixed and Free Quarterly*
    *Fixed and Free Anthology*
    *Storm Warning*
    *Green Left*
    *The Enchanted Circle News*
    *DISSENT anthology*
    *Revolutionary Poets Brigade Anthologies*
    *Veterans Against War online*
    *Special Forces Trust online*
    *Cultivating Voices Online*
    *Fungi Magazine*
    *KUMISS*
    *The Cornelian (Iona University)*
    *Dead Forever Anthology*
    *Reimagine America an Anthology for the Future*
    *Bayou Blues & Red Clay anthology*
    *Winter Solstice Poetry of Placitas New Mexico*
    *Central Avenue magazine and anthology*
    *The Rag*
    *Maple Leaf Anthology*
    *Quintessential Listening Poetry Online*
    *Sage Trail*
    *Adobe Walls*
    *Más Tequila Review Special Forces Charitable Trust online*
    *Maple Leaf Rag II*
    *Café Review*
    *Silence of the Messengers* (video-poem directed by Justin R Romine)

## Bio

Bill Nevins, born August 4, 1947, is a poet, a songwriter, a journalist, and a retired University of New Mexico educator who has worked in various media including film and video. Bill grew up in the US northeast and has lived in New Mexico since 1996. Bill graduated from Iona College, did graduate work in literature at U. of Connecticut and U. California at Berkeley and visited Ireland, Spain, Mexico, NYC, New Orleans and other places during both troubled and happier times. Bill is also a member of La Raza Unida, The National Writers Union, and Irish-American Writers and Artists.

bill_nevins@yahoo.com

www.ingramcontent.com/pod-product-compliance
Lightning Source LLC
Chambersburg PA
CBHW050848161224
19035CB00010B/127